And the World Stood Silent

And
the World
Stood Silent

Sephardic Poetry of the Holocaust

Translated and with commentaries by
Isaac Jack Lévy

University of Illinois Press
Urbana and Chicago

Illini Books edition, 2000
Manufactured in the United States of America
1 2 3 4 5 C P 5 4 3 2 1

∞ This book is printed on acid-free paper.

Library of Congress Cataloging-in-Publication Data

And the world stood silent : Sephardic poetry of the Holocaust /
   translated and with commentaries by Isaac Jack Lévy.
      p.   cm.
   Bibliography: p.
   Includes index.
   ISBN 0-252-01580-0 (alk. paper)
   ISBN 0-252-06861-0 (pbk. : alk. paper)
      1. Ladino poetry—Translations into English. 2. English poetry—
Translations from Ladino. 3. Holocaust, Jewish (1939–1945)—
Poetry. 4. Ladino poetry. I. Lévy, Isaac Jack.
   PC4813.7.A75   1989
   861′.62′080358—dc19   88-19932
                                                              CIP

To my people, the Sephardim, who, along
with millions of those of our faith,
have passed through suffering and death
out of loyalty to their birth.

Contents

Preface

In 1982 I read in the *Sephardic Home News* a letter by David Hyatt, president of the National Conference of Christians and Jews, concerning Rachel Dalven's play *A Testimonial to Life*, which deals with the Holocaust in Greece. Hyatt expressed his appreciation for being invited to the first reading of the play—in his words, "a little-known chapter of the Holocaust tragedy"—and his dismay that "very few people are aware of the fact that the Holocaust profoundly affected Athens and Greece."[1]

This was the first time that I had thought of the Holocaust in terms of the Sephardic literary tradition. For years I had carried out extensive research in Sephardic studies, but I had never fully realized the depth of the Sephardic literary and artistic expression in this area. I was not alone. My colleagues and fellow Sephardim also had neglected this poignant material, inadvertently ignoring the two primary forces behind Sephardic Holocaust poetry: the need to warn humanity and the duty to eulogize the victims.

In my research on Sephardic ballads, I had coincidentally collected a ballad that told of the Holocaust. It was sung to me in 1959 by Mrs. Stella Hasson, a victim of the concentration camps.[2] David F. Altabe told me about four poems composed by Yehuda Haim HaCohen Perahia during the Second World War while he was hiding in Greece from the Bulgarians and Germans. These had been found attached to the flyleaf of a booklet by Rafael Yosef Florentin, entitled *Kozas pasadas*, printed in Kavalla, Greece, in 1929.

I had always been aware of the Sephardic urge to express poetically inner feelings and reflections on daily activities. Whether in Rhodes, Tangier, New York, or Atlanta, I have come in contact with storekeepers, popular singers, and housewives who spontaneously composed songs to comment on national, communal, and family events. One of the most dramatic of my recollections is from the night of September 1, 1938, when the front-page news declared that the Jews of Rhodes must leave the island. Chelibon Maish immediately composed the song "Prima noche de septembre," which recounted the shattering revelations of this Sabbath eve. The song spread like wildfire through the Jewish quarter.

In the light of Hyatt's comments, I decided to undertake a reexamination of records and creative works among my people, the Sephardic community of Atlanta, Georgia, and of documents and tape recordings I had collected and stored since 1959. The results were astonishing. In a short span of a few weeks in Atlanta, I was able to locate numerous poetic texts pertaining to the Sephardic Holocaust. Among them was a nineteen-page work by Marcel Chalom, *Poèmes Juifs*, comprising both nationalistic and religious pieces. One selection is an elegy on the extermination of all but one member of his brother's family, and two others are in praise of a young survivor as the blessed remnant of the Chosen.[3] Mrs. Isaac Benshushan also made available to me a book that she received from South Africa, *Les martyrs Juifs de Rhodes et de Cos*, by Hizkia M. Franco. In his native Judeo-Spanish dialect, Franco unfolds his bereavement at the suffering of the Jewish communities of Rhodes and Cos and their subsequent extermination at the hands of "those civilized savages of Hitler's Germany."[4]

I was able to locate in my own library additional proof of the wealth of Sephardic oral and written compositions. Among such texts was the book of poems, *9 Eylûl: Poesias*, by the Turkish-born Esther Morguez Algrante, a journalist and highly respected author, and five issues of the Judeo-Spanish newspaper *El Tiempo*, given to me by Itzhak Ben Ruby, the editor, during my visit to Tel Aviv in 1968.[5] In these copies I discovered a long poem, "Listen My Brother," and an article commemorating the Jews of Salonika. I also found among the papers I had collected in Jerusalem in 1968 two anonymous poems, "Exile" and "Sacrifice."

With the support of the University of South Carolina, the Lucius N. Littauer Foundation, the Memorial Foundation for Jewish Culture, the Atlanta Jewish Federation, and some members of Or VeShalom Synagogue of Atlanta, Georgia, I continued my investigations in the United States and abroad. In 1982 I visited Israel, Greece, and Turkey. In the summer of 1983 I worked in the San Francisco area. I spent the summer of 1984 in Belgium, France, Greece, Holland, and Italy. During these trips I interviewed more than one hundred survivors as well as leaders of the communities devastated by the Holocaust and Sephardim who were not directly affected by the tragedy. In addition to the countries mentioned above, some of my sources came from Algeria, Bulgaria, Libya, and Tunisia.

I carried out extensive research in the libraries of the Ben Zvi and Yad Vashem institutes in Jerusalem, the Beit Hatefusoth (Museum of the Diaspora) in Tel Aviv, the Alliance Israëlite Universelle and the Centre de Documentation Juive Contemporaine in Paris, and the private holdings of some Sephardim. In Israel I also visited the museums of two kibbutzim, Lohamei Haghetaot and Yad Mordechai, where memorials have been built to the victims.

The response from the administrators of the organizations and from every individual was overwhelming. It was like a chain reaction. Each contributed experiences and volunteered the name of another possible source. My research yielded a great number of published and unpublished literary and artistic materials; a large quantity of photographs, slides, newspapers, and organizational accounts on the Greek, Libyan, and Tunisian communities; hundreds of hours of recordings on the experiences of the survivors of the camps; and leads to the few Christian and Sephardic painters and sculptors who have depicted scenes of the Sephardic phase of the Holocaust.

In my readings of the works on the Holocaust by scholars in the humanities and social sciences, I was quite perplexed to find that of the volumes I perused, few mention—and barely at that— the genocide undertaken by the Nazis against the Jewish populations in Italy, the Dodecanese Islands, Greece, and Tunisia and Libya. I was even more surprised to learn that very few Jewish historians and scholars were aware that the Holocaust affected the Sephardic communities. It is almost as if these Sephardim, who regard themselves as God's Chosen, did not belong to the Jewish nation.

In this volume I attempt to give voice to the forgotten Sephardim by allowing them to speak in their own words, through their poetry. Here emerge their life experiences, hopes, and aspirations. Here is traced the long journey to the concentration and extermination camps where they met their final destiny, along with millions of Jews and Christians.

NOTES

1. See also Lévy, "Holocaust Poetry."
2. This song first appeared in my master's thesis, "Sephardic Ballads and Songs in the United States."

3. Chalom, *Poèmes Juifs*, p. 7.

4. Franco, *Les martyrs Juifs*, pp. 117-18.

5. Ben Ruby was also a popular radio personality in Israel. He wrote several novels, including one that deals with the Holocaust, *El sekreto del mudo* (The secret of the mute), and numerous poems.

Acknowledgments

This book is the outcome of my close collaboration with many individuals and organizations. Had it not been for their unselfish contributions, this work would not have been possible.

First and foremost I wish to thank the poets and their family members for their generosity in allowing me to use their creations. I am also grateful to many of them for opening their homes to me and giving me the opportunity to interview them. Through the insights they shared with me as we spoke in Judeo-Spanish and French, I was able to reach a better understanding of the poems, and this enabled me to provide a more sensitive translation of these works.

Many friends and colleagues read the entire manuscript and provided constructive criticism. Even though we were not always in total accord, their arguments helped me to see different points of view. In particular I would like to acknowledge the late Professor Charles Lloyd of Davidson College for his daily encouragement, advice, and constructive criticism. A humanist and scholar, knowledgeable in several languages and in biblical and literary studies, Charles and I worked for many, many hours revising the manuscript. The time was made pleasant by his companionship and was lightened by his humor.

I must also acknowledge four scholars from the University of South Carolina: Professor Patricia Mason, for meticulously editing the original manuscript and generously offering many valuable insights into the translations of the poems, and for always being available when I needed help; Professor Freeman Henry, for his reading of every chapter, page after page, with much care; Professor Donald Greiner, for his insightful comments; and Professor John A. Bauer, for providing me with a printout of the music to "La vida de los Djudios en 1944."

I am appreciative of the help given to me by my good friend and rabbi, Howard Kosovski, in translation of Hebrew terms. He willingly shared with me his ideas regarding Jewish life and customs. Haham Dr. Solomon Gaon and Rabbi M. Mitchell Serels of the Jacob

E. Safra Institute of Sephardic Studies, Yeshiva University, were continuously supportive of my work, for which I am truly grateful.

And still, I owe this book to the help of more individuals than I can name: scholars, businessmen, housewives, community leaders, friends, relatives, and many others who brought to my attention records, documents, photographs, publications in scholarly journals and newspapers (no longer in circulation) from this country and abroad. In particular I would like to thank Mrs. Violette Mayo Fintz, a survivor of the camps who now resides in Capetown, South Africa, and Mr. Shelomo Reuven, originally from Salonika, who until his recent death lived in Tel Aviv. Over the years they provided me with materials and the names of other survivors and poets.

I am sincerely indebted to Judith McCulloh, executive editor at the University of Illinois Press, for her faith in this work. She has shown at all times a sensitive understanding of the topic and has given me her continuous support. I am especially grateful to Theresa L. Sears, associate editor, also at the University of Illinois Press, for her careful editing and fine suggestions which contributed greatly to the final form of the manuscript.

I am appreciative to the staff of the E. H. Little Library of Davidson College for locating reference works and to Professor Steven Lonsdale for typing the Greek poems and checking the translations. I wish also to thank Professor J. Gill Holland, a poet himself, for reading the poems.

I am truly grateful for the generous financial assistance awarded to me by the following organizations: the Provost's Fund and the Sponsored Program and Research Office of the University of South Carolina; the Lucius N. Littauer Foundation; the Atlanta Jewish Federation; the National Council of Jewish Culture; the Or Ve-Shalom Synagogue of Atlanta, Georgia; and the Southern Regional Education Board. The Sephardic Educational Center in Jerusalem, through its president, Dr. J. A. Nessim, has supported the publication of this work. This is especially important to me since this organization is committed to the perpetuation of Sephardic culture.

I wish to thank Professor Howard Schwartz for permitting me to reproduce an excerpt of the poem "Don't Show Me," by Ruth Baker, published in *Voices within the Ark* (New York, 1980). I am also thankful to Ms. Evelyne Kadouche and the *Tribune Juive* for allowing me to use the poem "Mon sang" (vol. 2, no. 5, March–April 1985). My gratitude as well to Alfred A. Knopf, Inc., for authorizing me to use four lines of Hanna Senech's "Blessed Is the Match," translated by Marie Syrkin, which appeared in London in 1948 in a book entitled *Blessed Is the Match: The Story of Jewish Resistance*.

Finally, I would like to express my gratitude to my wife and colleague, Professor Rosemary Lévy Zumwalt, for the time and energy she devoted to this project in all its phases. She provided me with invaluable assistance in the research, in interviewing the poets, and in translating some of the poems and editing the manuscript. Most of all, I am deeply grateful to her for the emotional support she gave me while I was working on these materials, which were like a ghost of my past and led to many painful recollections. She helped me through countless difficult moments with her strength and understanding.

A Note on the Translations

In translating the poetry, I have been guided by two concerns: that the feeling of the Sephardic poets be conveyed; and that the meaning be accurately represented. Mine are not literal, word-for-word translations. To be fair to the spirit of the poetry, I have attempted to follow the principles used by the first Sephardic translators of the Torah, in the *Bible in Two Columns, Hebraic and Spanish,* published in Amsterdam in 1762: "In the translation in the Spanish language, we search for the most appropriate word in the language in order to express the meaning of the text."

The task of translating from Judeo-Spanish is complicated by the lack of a definitive dictionary. Joseph Nehama, from Salonika, Greece, compiled an excellent Judeo-Spanish/French dictionary that greatly facilitated my work. Understandably, there are limitations in such an energetic undertaking that are linked to the lack of a standardized orthography and to the variations in pronunciation used by the Sephardim of different geographical regions. In fact, the compilation of a definitive dictionary might well be an impossible task. Judeo-Spanish has drawn vocabulary from Arabic, French, Greek, Hebrew, Italian, Turkish, and even English, as of late. Often the same word carries a different meaning in the two languages, such as *resentir,* "to be resentful or hurt" in Castilian and "to feel the effects, to experience" in the Judeo-Spanish of Salonika and Rhodes; or *genero,* meaning "type, class, genre" in Castilian and "son-in-law" in Judeo-Spanish, borrowed from the Italian. In the event that I could not translate a word or phrase, I sought the help of some of the poets who were still alive and members of the older generation living in the United States or abroad. I also relied heavily on my native knowledge of the language.

While some scholars have attempted to standardize the orthography of the written materials in Judeo-Spanish—an effort that has not been adopted systematically by the majority of scholars—I have chosen to remain faithful to the original sources in spelling, spacing, punctuation, and grammatical usage so as to represent the poets in their own voices. Problems, of course, attend this decision. There are differences in spelling, sometimes within the poetic corpus of one person or even within a single sentence. On occasion, even the name of the author appears with different spelling; for example, Algrante and Algranti. There are a number of reasons for this variation. First, the emphasis in Judeo-Spanish is mainly on oral tradition, which varies from one locale to another; hence, pronunciation, spelling, and vocabulary are influenced by other languages spoken in the particular region. Second, Judeo-Spanish is written with Hebrew characters—both in block letters and *Rashi*—which for certain words will offer two alternatives in the use of the vowels: for instance, the Hebrew "vov" could be transliterated either as "o" or "u" and the Hebrew "yod" as "i" or "e." Third, educational background—that is, whether the poet studied under the French or Italian system—influences both the choice of spelling and the use of accents.

A Brief History of the Sephardim

To understand how the Jews of Sephardic tradition were affected by the Holocaust, and before embarking on a thematic study of the poetry and on the presentation of original poems and their English translations, we must first know something about the Sephardim, once the pride and glory of the Jewish nation.[1] Several theories have been advanced on the origin of the term "Sepharad," mentioned in the Book of Obadiah, verse 20, as the Prophet speaks of those Hebrews in foreign lands: "and the captivity of Jerusalem, which is in Sepharad, shall possess the cities of the South." While some scholars propose the capital of Lydia, Sfard—now Sardis—as the birthplace of the Sephardim, others claim that the root of *sefard* derives from ". . . the legendary Garden of Hesperides (s-p-r-d) which was part of Hispanic Mauritania."[2] For political reasons, or for lack of a better nomenclature, the term "Sephardim" has been wrongfully used since the birth of the state of Israel to denote, if not all of the non-Ashkenazic branches of Judaism, at least the natives of North Africa as well as the Jews of Asia and the Near East.

Suffice it to say that the majority of scholars agree that the Sephardim are the direct descendants of Jews of the Iberian Peninsula who established themselves in the northwestern countries of Europe and in those countries bordering the Mediterranean basin. Their native tongue, even after hundreds of years of exile from Spain by the Inquisition of 1492, is Judeo-Spanish, called by some Ladino or Judezmo. In their exodus from Portugal and Spain—countries they loved and esteemed as a Second Jerusalem in spite of the tortures and pogroms that befell them at the hands of the Inquisition—they retained the customs and folklore nurtured by their ancestors on the peninsula even before the Roman conquest.

"Sephardic" is more than a linguistic or geographical designation. If we were to ask Spanish Jews what Sepharad stands for, their faces would light up with pride and they would say that it is "a way of life; one that has existed for over 2000 years with all its glories, its traditions, its beliefs. More precisely . . . : 'It is a rich legacy of religion, culture, language, art, science—the story of a noble people and heroic figures—people who endured the Inquisition of Spain, who sailed to the New World with Columbus, colonized eastern Brazil in 1695, fought the first fight for civil rights on American soil.' "[3] Centuries later, they would add, the Sephardic people migrated by force or by choice to other lands and once again contributed vigorously to many sectors of the social, political, and economic life of North and South America, of Africa, and of Europe and the Near East. Sadly, they would recall that while the Sephardim enjoyed long periods of peace and acceptance in most countries, they also suffered the prejudices and persecutions of the local peoples, culminating in the tragedy of the Holocaust, which annihilated tens of thousands of their coreligionists and destroyed their cities, like Salonika, the "City and Mother of Israel," as it was known for its glorious achievements.

Legends tell us that the Jews, seeking to improve their condition, arrived in Spain as early as the reign of King Solomon. They settled in towns and became an integral part of the Iberian population. Notwithstanding their financial and political assistance to the kingdom of the Goths, the Jews found it necessary to withdraw into ghettos (juderías) to avoid the many persecutions, under both the Romans and the Visigoths, who often forced them to embrace Christianity and in some instances sold them as slaves.

In A.D. 711 the Jews helped the conquering forces from North Africa that were headed by the Muslim Tarik, said to be of Jewish ancestry. Under Arab rule they were given greater liberties and shared in the administration of the country as ministers of police, ministers of finance, and prime ministers. Some Jews even held the title of prince. With the exception of a few short, brutal periods under the fanatic Almoravides and Almohades, they fared well on the peninsula, in an atmosphere of freedom and with few restrictions imposed upon them. They participated in the cultural and economic activities of the country and, together with the Arabs, advanced in all phases of contemporary culture. Among them one can count astronomers, astrologers, botanists, pharmacologists, and physicians; literary, religious, and historical writers; philosophers and rabbis. To this list must be added the universally renowned humanist Maimonides. Because of their scientific and intellectual accomplishments, these Jews were sought out by both Arabs and Christians, who vied for their services.

Under these propitious conditions, the splendor of Moslem Spain was enhanced by the arrival of Jews from the Orient, who also made economic, literary, and scientific contributions to their new home. With their coreligionists they virtually monopolized all banking and commercial transactions, silk commerce, and a significant share of the trade with Asia.[4] They populated the most famous cities of the peninsula, such as Toledo, the "City of Generations," with an estimated population of 70,000 Jews in the thirteenth century. Toledo was the cultural nucleus of scientific, literary, and rabbinic investigations—the Jerusalem of the medieval Hebrews in Spain.

Most Jewish leaders and intellectuals living in Christian lands retaken from the Moors also enjoyed the highest respect and admiration of the ruling class. It is true that the masses, the clergy, and some of the nobility tried to undermine Jewish commercial and political competency. However, such monarchs as Don Pedro the Cruel availed themselves of their services and placed them in offices of great importance. The *yeshivas* and rabbinic courts in northern Spain were as important in the Jewish communities outside the peninsula as were those in the Arab sectors. Without a doubt, there was a considerable influence of the Spanish Jews on other nations. Their knowledge spread to practically all European countries as well as to Turkey, Egypt, the Near East, and many other lands.

A major concern of scholars in recent years has been the contribution of the Jews and crypto-Jews to the shaping of Spanish civilization. Up to 1390 the Jews considered themselves to be secure, in spite of local accusations and harangues. Beginning in March of 1391, however, outrages spread from Seville to Cordoba, Toledo, Segovia, Burgos, Valencia, Barcelona, the Balearic Islands, and all corners of Spain. The campaign against the Jews, which a century later led to their expulsion, was already in full swing; and the extermination of Spanish Jewry could not be contained. The *juderías* were ransacked and put to the torch. Thousands were forced to convert or were tortured to death. Not all of those who embraced Catholicism were sincere in the new faith, accepting baptism only as a means of survival. At first the new Christians enjoyed all the privileges of the land and held the most prestigious offices in the royal court, the army, the church, and academic institutions. Eventually, they too experienced the same problems as their forebears. The new attacks were the result of social, economic, and political jealousies and natural calamities, rather than exclusively religious fanaticism. Hardly anyone was spared, even when popes, monarchs, local leaders, and the inquisitors themselves intervened on their behalf. As in the case of the Holocaust, the annals of the Inquisition show that the horrendous acts—penitence, imprisonment, torture, burning, exhumation—were not limited to the Judaizers (secret Jews) but also affected Moriscos, Lutherans, and Huguenots, as well as sincere converts to Christianity. By inhuman edicts and exploits, the peninsula deprived itself of the help of such useful and industrious subjects.

Once ejected from their homes in August of 1492 by order of the Catholic monarchs, many of the banished, realizing that it would be better for their physical and political well-being, emigrated to the Near East, especially to the Ottoman Empire and its territories, which were governed by liberal-minded rulers, and to North Africa. Some Jews settled also in Bulgaria, Romania, Yugoslavia, and even in Jerusalem and Safed. A later wave of New Christian converts, desiring to return to Judaism, took refuge in Holland, England, and some cities of Germany and eastern Europe.

The Sephardim were welcomed by the sovereigns of these countries. Sultan Biazit II of Turkey was proud to adopt this wandering people as his own, for he realized that Spain's loss would be Turkey's gain. Suleiman the Magnificent also encouraged the immigration of wealthy, cultured Spanish and Portuguese Marranos. In time we find those who accepted Christianity to escape the Inquisition, as well as the nonconverts, in the cultural centers of Amsterdam, Vienna, and Salonika, and in the Italian courts and the Turkish palaces. Neither sorrow nor religious and racial uprisings, which inevitably haunted them wherever they settled, would impede their full participation in the academic, scientific, and political spheres. Baruch Spinoza in Holland, Abrabanel in Italy, and Amatus Lusitanus in Belgium and Salonika were representative of the future descendants of Spanish Jews. The Spanish and Portuguese Marranos, as well as the Augustinian, Franciscan, and Dominican monks of Jewish origin, who took refuge in Holland founded academies that rivaled those of the Iberian poets and dramatists.[5] By their efforts Holland developed the Dutch merchant marine and the city of Amsterdam became wealthy in money and in intellectual pursuits.

Pride of ancestry, anxiety to preserve the family fortune, feelings of superiority in their public and private lives, and a sense of martyrdom forced the western Sephardim to inbreed and to refuse intermarriage with Ashkenazic Jews. There were other social and cultural factors that contributed to the maintenance of bondages, such as language and variations in ritual, and these also caused the decline of the group. Moreover, the ultimate break with the Hispanic world, the desire of the scientists, economists, and humanists to rival their Christian compatriots, and their hope to participate fully in the politics of the Western countries in which they resided eventually led the Sephardim to abandon Spanish and Portuguese as their domestic tongue, along with most of their former traditions. The Sephardic *hidalgos* "were not eager to rejuvenate themselves when, voluntarily, thousands and even millions of Ashkenazic Jews arrived in their countries."[6] In time they were overwhelmed by their Germanic and Slavic brethren, who reaped the fruit of Sephardic labor. Thus, this segment of Spanish and Portuguese Jewry, by its own actions, divorced itself from the pan-Sephardic world, not necessarily from the religious and historical aspect, but from the traditional way of life that has been faithfully preserved up to this day by their counterparts in the Levant.

Unlike their northern brethren, the Jews and Marranos who adopted Greece and the Ottoman Empire as their homes retained their language and traditions from Spain. While there was a high level of education among the pre-Sephardic Romaniot Jewish population of Greece, and among the Ashkenazic rabbis of Salonika who fled persecution in northern Europe, still the newcomers from the Iberian Peninsula felt a sense of superiority. Their pride of ancestry and education helped them build a new way of life by intermingling some of the traditions of their new homes with those of Spain and Portugal. Their talents and efficiency in many areas of endeavor earned for them protective decrees not enjoyed previously by the local Jews nor by any other minority. They soon established centers such as Salonika, which, as Toledo and Lucena had in years past, earned the designation of a "Jewish republic," a self-sustaining city in northern Greece rivaling the cultural centers of Italy and the leading commercial centers of Ancona and Venice. The Sephardim continued to play an important role as bankers, merchants, and scholars. The Jews of Salonika practically monopolized the woolen cloth industry, believed to have been brought from Spain.

Wherever they settled—Salonika, Istanbul, Smyrna, Monastir, Rhodes, Sarajevo—these Jews steadfastly retained their language and their traditions from Spain and Portugal. The newcomers created self-sufficient groups according to their place of origin—Aragon, Castile, Catalonia, Seville, Toledo—a custom quite often duplicated in the twentieth century by their descendants who emigrated to Africa, the Americas, and elsewhere in search of more favorable economic circumstances. In turn they named their synagogues after their former homes—Monastir, Istanbul, Rhodes—wherein monocracy, not theocracy, became the basis of authority. Officers were democratically elected to rule, in conjunction with the rabbinate, the spiritual, educational, judicial, and economic aspects of their existence. The Sephardim generally governed with leniency, objectivity, and wisdom, but when necessary they had recourse to social pressures and invoked the *herem* (excommunication) on any dissenters. This form of popular government, which ruled according to biblical and Talmudic laws and with specific up-to-date written ordinances, continued to exist until the Second World War among groups in North Africa, Asia Minor, and the Dodecanese Islands.

Contrary to general belief, once settled in their new locations the Sephardim did not live isolated from their brethren in other lands or from their Spanish homeland. For many years they remained in contact with converted relatives who still resided in Spain and Portugal, and they kept in touch with the culture and folklore of their former homes through acquaintances in Italy and through their interactions with travelers. The interconnection of the Sephardic communities of Turkey, Greece, Italy, Portugal, Spain, France, England, the Low Countries, North Africa, and Asia Minor, as well as those in the New World, was due to family relationships, common economic interests, and cultural attachments.

However ideal this mode of living may have been, the Sephardim residing in Christian countries fell victim to the prejudices and envy of the local inhabitants. Abraham Galanté has identified at least forty-four cases of ritual murders alleged to have taken place on the island of Rhodes since 1521, when that island was ruled by the Knights of St. John. As will be pointed out later in this study, the Jews of Salonika also suffered at the hands of the Greek population once the city was taken over from the Ottoman Empire.

The jealousy of the people, the blindness and fanaticism of the clergy, and the ignorance of the masses in whatever land the Sephardim found themselves brought back memories of the past—recollections of the Spanish dungeons where they had been destined to rot or to end their lives as human torches. Still the Sephardim held fast to their convictions, since they well knew that the fate of Israel is one of settling and banishment, of success and failure, of being strangers in all lands. The wheels of misfortune did not spare the descendants from Spain in the twentieth century, when Balkan nationalism and increasingly adverse economic conditions, military conscription, and parental restraint caused the majority of the younger generation, especially those from poor families, to migrate to France, Palestine, South America, the Belgian Congo, Rhodesia, and the United States. Advancement was not easy; it required much hard work merely to survive in these countries and to support relatives back home. Wherever they went, the Sephardim encountered many obstacles. Their knowledge of Judeo-Spanish, Turkish, French, Greek, and Italian did not help them to communicate in their new surroundings or to obtain positions of responsibility. Their unfamiliarity with Yiddish separated them from the rest of Jewry, who frequently asked, "If you don't speak Yiddish, how can you be a Jew?" Forced to live an isolated, clannish existence, surviving in an austere environment, the twentieth-century immigrants began by holding menial jobs. However, with better educational and business opportunities, later generations of Sephardim prospered.

Since the Second World War there have been few areas of human endeavor in which the members of the Sephardic family have not participated. Unfortunately, unlike previous generations of Levantine Jews, the inevitable social, economic, and linguistic assimilation with the local populace is resulting in a break with the past. Whether in Europe, the Americas, Africa, or Israel, the Sephardim today are destined finally to relinquish their traditional way of life and adapt to the dominant tradition of the community and country in which they reside. It seems that nothing can stop the historic absorption and inevitable elimination of this ethnic group. (An exception, temporary though it might be, is in Israel, where concentrated numbers of Sephardim have been able to maintain their way of life, though even there the trend is toward assimilation, toward a new identity as Israelis). In France, Belgium, Turkey, and the United States, I have encountered children who do not know the language, the narrative tradition, the customs, or the foodways. One must acknowledge that there are academic and cultural groups in France, Greece, Israel, Spain, the United States, and, to a lesser extent, countries in Ibero-

America and South Africa that have been recording and documenting the Judeo-Spanish tradition. Still, the identity of the people as Sephardim is diminishing.

This brief history would be incomplete without mentioning the total and swift destruction of the Sephardic communities in Bulgaria, Greece, the Dodecanese Islands, Tunisia, and Libya by the Third Reich and its collaborators. The crimes committed against the Sephardim were the same as those directed against their Ashkenazic coreligionists. For the Nazis, the crucial consideration was the extinction of the Jewish people, regardless of place of origin or nationality. For instance, the Jews residing in France who were citizens of neutral countries, such as Switzerland, Turkey, and Spain, were not spared; they too were collected and deported to concentration camps. The Jewish citizens from Bulgaria and Romania—satellite nations belonging to the Axis—who lived in foreign countries were not exempted from the deportation by the Germans, even though they were protected in their own nations.

It is difficult to ascertain the total pre–World War II population of Sephardic Jews in the countries involved in the Holocaust because in most European nations they lived among the Ashkenazim. According to Haim Vidal Sephiha, who quotes other sources, 60,000 Sephardim lived in France, 3,000 in Belgium, 2,000 in Holland, 5,000 in Germany, and 15,000 in Austria. However, these reports do not take into account how many Sephardim emigrated prior to the Nazi persecutions in Germany and Austria.[7]

Few figures have been provided that separate the deportees of the non-Balkan states and North African countries according to their place of origin and ethnicity; and even when these numbers are given, it is impossible to determine exact percentages. For instance, studying the table compiled by Georges Etlin, which is furnished by Serge Klarsfeld in *Le mémorial de la déportation des Juifs de France*, one can be almost sure of the Sephardic origin of the Jews from Bulgaria (140), Greece (1,499), Turkey (1,282), Egypt (27), Lebanon (2), and Syria (17), and perhaps even those from Portugal (19) and Spain (145); however, this deals only with deportations from Drancy. The figures given for the rest of the Balkan countries, western Europe, and the Americas do not solve the problem since all those deported from France are grouped together. Beate Klarsfeld states that the table is not complete. Additionally, my informants in Salonika and Israel report that over 5,000 Salonikan Jews living in France were transported to the eastern camps, rather than the 1,499 reported by Etlin.[8] This is supported by Isaac Aruh (no. 124338), a survivor from Auschwitz, who, upon his liberation, communicated to Miriam Novitch, author and curator of Kibbutz Lohamei Haghetaot, that he learned in Salonika of the deportation from France of 5,000 Salonikan Jews in November 1942.[9] Perhaps this figure is somewhat inflated; however, when I visited Paris during the summer of 1984, I was told by a member of the Sephardic Federation that many more than 2,000 Salonikan Jews were involved in the deportations.

The Jewish communities of the Balkans, the Dodecanese Islands, and North African countries were mainly Sephardic, and one can arrive at a more reliable estimate of those affected. Thus, this survey of Sephardic victims of the Holocaust will concentrate on these countries.

Like the Ashkenazim, the Sephardim suffered discriminatory legislation during the period of the Holocaust: curfew, confiscation of property, declaration of possessions, registration with local authorities, and wearing of the yellow star. Sadistic beatings, endless hours of calisthenics, loss of jobs, payment of large ransoms and fines, restriction of movement, frequent executions, and service in the forced labor camps were common. Systematic roundups and deportations of people in boxcars to Auschwitz, Buchenwald, Bergen Belsen, Birkenau, Dachau, Maidanek, Sobibor, Treblinka, and many labor camps began as early as 1940. Of the six million Jews who perished, at least 160,000 were Sephardim, a figure that includes a large percentage of the Jewish population in the Balkans and the Dodecanese Islands. The Sephardim, too, were eliminated by disease, hunger, cold, firing squads, drowning in the Danube River and the Aegean Sea, gas chambers, and crematoria. Complete Sephardic centers were literally destroyed. Some 80 percent of the Jewish population of Greece perished—only 10,026 of 75,477 survived the Holocaust—with the hardest blow taken by Macedonia and Thrace, which, together with Salonika, lost over 97 percent of their Jewish population. Today, approximately 6,000 Jews still live in Greece.

Greece was divided into three zones of occupation. The northern zone, specifically the Yugoslavian section of Macedonia, Greek Thrace, and Romanian Dobrudja, was seized by Bulgaria, one of three nations to have signed in March of 1941 the Tripartite Pact with Germany, thus becoming formal allies. The rest of the northern part of Greece was occupied by Germany, and the southern zone was under Italian rule.

As soon as the German forces entered Salonika on April 9, 1941, they began the expropriation of properties, including thousands of books and religious artifacts from renowned libraries and synagogues. Most of the local Jewish leaders were arrested, and life became unbearable in the community once referred to with pride as the "Jewish Republic of Salonika." By the middle of 1942, some 5,500 Salonikan Jews were forced into labor camps in various parts of Greece. The Germans were constantly demanding exorbitant ransoms, which at first the community managed to pay through great effort and deprivation—as one of the Sephardic leaders stated: "It was money or their life." In one instance, to save those detained the community paid three billion drachmas to the Germans, who then refused to release the detainees. When the community could not meet the demand for a huge sum to prevent the expropriation of the historic Jewish cemetery, the Germans took possession on December 6, 1942, and used the tombstones to line a swimming pool for German troops and for the construction of Greek homes. The Greek Orthodox cemetery, located only a few yards away, was not touched. Jewish youths, many who had served bravely in the war against Italy, were mobilized into work groups and forced to drain swamps and build roads and fortifications.

On February 6, 1943, the SS arrived in Salonika to implement the racial laws of Nuremberg. After the internment of the Jews in designated zones, the deportations began on March 15, 1943, and continued until August 7, 1943, when the last train left Salonika. The National Liberation Front (EAM) saved over a thousand Jews from being deported, and another few hundred members of the community were spared either because they held Spanish or Italian passports or because they were members of Greek partisan groups. Approximately one thousand deportees survived the death camps of Poland and Germany.

The Jews who lived in the Italian sector of Greece fared much better. The Italian government refused to deport them, in spite of the constant demands from their German allies, and more than once Italian officials issued passes to Jews from other Greek areas to cross into their zone. It was not until Italy surrendered to the Allies in September of 1943 that the Germans occupied the southern region of Greece and the Dodecanese Islands. Then, under the Germans, the nightmare began for the 10,000 or more Jews living in Athens, Patras, Janina, Larisa, Volos, Kastoria, and other cities on mainland Greece and the islands.

The Jewish people of Athens and the Greek peninsula were integrated into Greek life. Their language was mainly Greek, not Judeo-Spanish as in Salonika, and their residences were dispersed throughout the cities. Having learned of the disaster that befell the Jews of Salonika, Macedonia, and Thrace, the Jewish leaders of Athens saved thousands of lives by destroying the required list of names and addresses of all Jews living in the city. Moreover, the Jews of the southern region were actively assisted by the local Greek inhabitants and received the protection of Archbishop Damaskinos and the Greek Orthodox church. Archbishop Chrysostomos and Mayor Lukos Karrer of Zante alerted them of the forthcoming deportation and sent 195 Jews to the remote villages of the island for protection. In spite of the archbishop's threat to join the remaining 62 Jews at the port of embarkation, the Gestapo proceeded with the deportation. Ironically, the boat from Corfu that was to have removed the Jews from Zante was full and they were left behind.

The Jewish and Greek members of the National Liberation Front, along with other underground groups and the Greek Orthodox church, sheltered the Jewish population of the southern region. Through their efforts a great number of Jews went into hiding in villages, monasteries, and convents; among them were members of my own family. The Resistance even helped some Jews to escape to Turkey and Palestine.[10] It should also be noted that the Spanish and Portuguese governments played a great part in the rescue of the Sephardim from Greece and other western European countries.[11] Those Jews who did not heed the warnings suffered the same fate as their northern co-religionists. Some 7,000 were deported from this region of Greece; of these, approximately 250 survived the camps.

On May 21, 1944, the Gestapo arrested the Jews of Hania and Rethymnon, in Crete, and on June 4 transported them to Heraklion, where 400 Greek Orthodox civilians and 300 Italian prisoners of war, held as hostages, joined them for the long trip to the concentration camps. Only 120 miles away, between the islands of Melos and Polegandros, the ship was intentionally sunk. According to L. S. Stavrianos, only seven Jews from Crete survived the war by hiding; 98 percent of the Jews on the island died.[12]

The role of Bulgaria in the Holocaust is a strange one. In spite of the constant demands of its German allies to proceed with the final solution, Bulgaria refused to deport any of the 50,000 Jewish citizens living in what came to be known as Old Bulgaria (as opposed to New Bulgaria, which was made up of the territories seized in 1941 after the signing of the Tripartite Pact with Hitler's Germany). The Jews of Bulgaria had led a relatively secure life ever since pre-Roman times. They were well received and highly respected by the local peoples, even though anti-Semitism was not totally absent, especially during the last decades of the nineteenth century. During the Second World War, anti-Jewish laws were enacted and approximately 10,000 Jews were forced to build highways and railways. The wearing of the yellow star was at first mandatory; some refused to obey the order, while others wore it proudly. Jews were not allowed to own a business or earn a living, and their property was expropriated. Resettlements were common. Still, King Boris III, church leaders, and members of the Bulgarian Parliament objected to the deportations of the Jews of Old Bulgaria.[13] Hundreds of Jews holding foreign passports were allowed to sail for Palestine. Unfortunately, the boat—named *Salvador* (Savior)—which was both unseaworthy and overloaded, sank in the Sea of Marmara.

The Jews of New Bulgaria were less fortunate. Bulgaria had acquiesced on February 22, 1943, to the German demands for the deportation of all the Jews from the newly annexed territories. Approximately 5,000 Jews from Thrace were placed in boxcars for the long journey to the camps. At the Bulgarian town of Lom, they were transferred onto river barges for the trip up the Danube. Martin Gilbert states that, due to the horrible conditions, several hundred died before reaching Treblinka.[14] Vicki Tamir records an account by an eyewitness that the Germans overturned the barges: "And the blue waters of [the] Danube proved as accommodating as any crematorium. No one survived. No one returned. There is no record of the arrival of this particular transport at any German concentration camp."[15]

In March 1943 the Bulgarians turned their attention to the Macedonian Jews of Bitola, Skopje, Shipt, and Pirot. To prevent escapes, soldiers sealed the Albanian border while the police herded the Jews into tobacco warehouses or escorted them to railway stations. The internees were robbed of their possessions, many were forced to undress and were sadistically beaten, and women were brutally raped.

Between March 22, 1943, and March 29, 1943, over 8,000 Jews from Macedonia were sent in three transports to Treblinka. None survived.

While Germany had no difficulty convincing Bulgaria to deport the Jews from the acquired territories, it failed to extract the same agreement from its Italian allies. This was a cause of frustration, as one can tell from this entry in Joseph Goebbels's diary: "The Italians are extremely lax in the treatment of the Jews. They protect the Italian Jews both in Tunis and in occupied France."[16] The Italians did more than harbor their own citizens. In the nations they seized—Albania, Greece, France, Yugoslavia, Tunisia—and in their own land and territories—Italy, Libya, the Dodecanese Islands—Jews found a haven from Nazi persecutions, even though still subject to anti-Jewish laws. In 1938 the foreign Jews living in Italy and the Dodecanese Islands were ordered to leave the country; some Italian leaders requested the expulsion of all Jews.[17] Eventually, additional laws were enacted excluding Jews from the armed forces and civic jobs; limitations were set on owning property, and intermarriages were forbidden. I recall seeing my family in Rhodes read in the newspaper about the antiracial laws and the expulsion order. Even though I was a young child and could not understand what was happening, I was struck by their sad expressions on that Friday eve as we sat down to eat the Sabbath meal. Fear gripped the Jewish quarters. Tormented by the thought of leaving family, friends, and possessions behind, an important Jewish leader committed suicide by throwing himself, hands in his pants pockets, into the sea.

Unlike the foreign Jews in Italy proper and those in Libya, the Dodecanese Jews were neither interned nor arrested. Life changed considerably, however. Many of us left the islands in 1939 for Central and South African countries and Tangier, Morocco, which was an international city. The Jews who remained on the islands were to some extent protected by the officials of the Italian government and the army against the anti-Semitism of the Greek population. No harm came to them, as was the case with the Jews in Italy and those under Italian occupation. Laws were drawn in such a way that they did not apply to a large segment of the Jewish population. The Italian people, officials of the Catholic church, and members of the armed forces, as well as the royal family, were not eager to join their German allies in persecuting and deporting Jews to the death camps.

With Italy's surrender to the Allies on September 8, 1943, German troops took over Italian possessions. On September 23, orders were given to begin the deportations. Roundups began immediately and no area was excluded. By the spring of 1944, several thousand Italian Jews were sent to concentration camps, yet many more were able to save themselves by leaving the country or hiding in Catholic homes. The SS spared no financial or human resources to annihilate the Jews. Even though the war was turning against them and the German military was being defeated on all fronts, the Germans, when retreating from Greece, chose to leave their weaponry behind and load the trains with the Jews of the Dodecanese Islands.

On July 18, 1944, the roundup of the Jews of Rhodes took place. Over 1,700 were interned in the Aviation Palace, where their possessions were confiscated; 39 Jews who carried Turkish passports were saved by the Turkish consul general, Selahettin Bey. On July 23, 1944, the Jews of Rhodes were transported, without food or water, to Piraeus on three small petrol tankers which stopped in Cos to pick up 94 additional deportees. By the time they reached the island of Leros, all were sick and weak with hunger. The captain, an Austrian, refused to proceed until provisions were brought aboard. Once on the mainland, SS officers held the Jews for four days without any food in Haydar, a camp near Athens. The guards abused them and took whatever valuables they still had in their possession. The long journey to Auschwitz began on August 3, a slow, excruciating trip that took approximately twenty more days. It is reported that 22 Jews died in the tankers, at the port of Piraeus, in Haydar, and in the crowded boxcars. The Jewish communities of Rhodes, which had been known as "Little Jerusalem," and Cos came to an end. Both islands, according to legend and biblical accounts, had been populated by Jews since the time of King Solomon.

The roundup and extermination of Jews were not limited to Europe. In Tunisia, a French protectorate, and Libya, an Italian colony, Jews also fell victim to the Nazis. M. Mitchell Serels comments: "Not content to fight the advancing Allied forces, the Germans turned their attention to the [50,000] Jews."[18] An *Einsatzkommando* group of SS and police were dispatched in November of 1942 to solve the Jewish problem. In spite of the protests of Admiral Esteva, the résident général, the first Jewish arrests took place on November 23. Among those seized was the president of the community, Mr. Borgel, who, after the others were released on November 29, was made responsible for the behavior of the Jews and ordered to report to German headquarters twice a day. Soon after, SS Colonel Walter Rauff was charged by General Von Nehring to form a nine-member council, at first presided over by the chief rabbi, to take care of all Jewish affairs vis-à-vis the German government. Members of the French police as well as anti-Jewish military officers of the Vichy government were only too eager to assist the Germans in carrying out their demands against the Jewish population.

Tunisian Jews were subjected to anti-Jewish decrees, which limited their movements and the performance of their professions, and the wearing of the yellow star was instituted. The Germans also disbanded Jewish organizations and forbade the printing of newspapers. Life became intolerable in the northern sector, as it was occupied by the Germans. The Nazis systematically took hostages, imposed heavy fines, demanded property, plundered the Jewish stores and quarters, and murdered and beat the Jews; they constantly requisitioned monies, clothing, furniture, and, before leaving Tunisia, demanded fifty kilos of gold. During this period of terror the Germans enslaved over 4,000 Jews between the ages of eighteen and twenty-eight. They were mobilized as forced laborers in the harbors and on railway projects, as well as on roads, the front lines, and airfields; 2,575 of them succumbed from exhaustion, hunger, maltreatment, and Allied bombardments.

While interviewing several Tunisian immigrants in Tel Aviv in 1982, I was informed by a survivor of one of the labor camps that the Germans had utilized the existing cement factories in Tunisia to begin the construction of death camps, since they realized that mass deportations to the European death centers were not feasible. Had it not been for the lack of railway lines, roads, and the Allied occupation of Tunisia in the spring of 1943, the destruction of Tunisian Jewry would have been achieved. As it was, several Jewish leaders were arrested and deported by air to Auschwitz, Buchenwald, and other European camps. A family of three was decapitated.[19]

Under the Italians, the Jewish population of Libya was also subject to discriminatory measures. Jewish organizations were ordered to cease their activities, and at the instigation of the mufti of Jerusalem, local Arab officials, and the German diplomatic corps, young Arabs in Benghazi and other Middle Eastern countries attacked the Jews.[20] Although British forces briefly occupied Benghazi in 1941, the Germans reoccupied it in February of 1942 and proceeded systematically to assault the Jewish population and harass Jewish business establishments. The Nazis swiftly transported 2,600 Jews to the southern city of Giado to build roads, where it is said that over 500 died of starvation and typhus. In April of the same year a new law decreed that Jews had to declare their property. Approximately 1,800 members of the community, between the ages of eighteen and forty-five, were sent to camps and forced to lay rails between Libya and Egypt. Dr. Isaac Menasche, a Salonikan Jew who survived internment in Bergen Belsen, informed me in 1982 that while in the camp he came into contact with many Jewish deportees from Libya who held British passports.

The Sephardim of Algeria and of Spanish and French Morocco did not suffer the same oppressions. The Jews in the international zone of Tangier, including my family, which had taken refuge in the city in 1939 to escape the discriminatory laws of Rhodes, carried on a normal life, even if at times it was difficult. However, the Algerian and Moroccan Jews who resided in the German-occupied zone of France and in the unoccupied Vichy provinces were declared "foreign." They were arrested by the Gestapo and the French police and deported in several convoys to the east, along with 85,000 to 90,000 Jews living in France.

The catastrophe that befell the Sephardim from Europe and North Africa at the hands of Nazi Germany and its local collaborators resulted in a total destruction of their way of life. In addition to the great number who perished in the death camps, the final outcome of World War II was the complete dissolution of the Sephardic and Romaniot communities. Haham Dr. Solomon Gaon speaks of the greatness of their communities, in *yeshivot*, in libraries, in language (Judeo-Spanish), in literature and art, as well as in social, spiritual, and cultural resources. The Sephardim, unlike their forebears who emigrated from the Iberian Peninsula, did not make any effort to duplicate their centers once in their new homes.[21] Indeed, although they retained aspects of their culture, such as religious rituals, language, folklore, and culinary traditions from their country of origin, still their main preoccupation was their immediate financial and physical well-being, not the pursuit of their communal life.

Failing to recognize, several decades later, one of his students who had survived the concentration camps, Haham Gaon was reminded by him: "It is not the 50 years of absence that makes recognition difficult, but we are now different people. . . . The Nazis have not merely destroyed our parents and families, but also our way of life. We are living in cemeteries and memories."[22]

NOTES

1. Portions of this chapter have been drawn from Lévy, "The Sephardim," pp. 1–12.

2. Besso, "Recent Theories," p. 14. For his comprehensive study of the definition of Sephardim, see pp. 13–18.

3. Lévy, "The Sephardim," p. 1. Part of this statement appears in "In Our Hands: The Sephardic Heritage," a pamphlet published by the Sephardic Studies Program of Yeshiva University.

4. Lévy, "The Sephardim," p. 2.

5. Besso, *Dramatic Literature*, p. 18.

6. Benardete, *Hispanic Culture*, pp. 32–33.

7. See Sephiha, *L'agonie des Judéo-Espagnols*, p. 5

8. See Klarsfeld, *Le mémorial de la déportation*. See also Klarsfeld, *Additif au mémorial*.

9. Novitch, *Le passage des Barbares*, p. 25.

10. For a more detailed account, see Stavrianos, "The Jews of Greece." For a comparative study dealing with the actions taken by the different Jewish leaders in Greece, see Ben, "Jewish Leadership in Greece."

11. See Avni, "Spanish Nationals in Greece." See also Avni, *Spain, the Jews and Franco*.

12. Stavrianos, "The Jews of Greece," p. 264.

13. Romania and Spain also protested the application of anti-Jewish laws for their own nationals.

14. Gilbert, *The Fate of the Jews*, pp. 124–25.

15. Tamir, "Bulgaria," p. 39. A pamphlet published in 1984 by the Jewish Museum of Greece, entitled "The Jews of Greece," offers both possibilities. Nikos Stavroulakis, the curator, writes on page 8: ". . . there is a good possibility that they were in fact drowned in the Danube." Yehuda Haim Perahia, in the commentary to his poem "The First Cry in Anguish," states, "On the night of March 3 and 4, 1943, the Bulgarians took all the Jews from Xeres, Drama, Kavalla, Xanthi, Cumulgina, and Dedeagatch and carried them to Bulgaria and from there to the Danube where, so they say, they drowned them."

16. Quoted in Gilbert, *The Holocaust*, p. 505.

17. For the attitude of the Italians toward Jews and Christians, both in Italy and occupied territories, see Zuccotti, *The Italians and the Holocaust*.

18. Serels, "The Non-European Holocaust," p. 112. Several themes are treated in the Gaon and Serels collection, including the role of Spain in protecting the Sephardim in France and the Holocaust as it affected the Jewish communities of Salonica, Janina, Morocco, Tunisia, Holland, Yu-

goslavia, and Rhodes. Also included is an article entitled "Holocaust in the Middle East: Iraq and the Mufti of Jerusalem."

19. For further information concerning the Jews from Tunisia, see Sabile, "Les Juifs de Tunisie." The December 1948 issue of *Le Monde Juif* also includes articles on the prelude of the deportations of Jews from France and the situation of the Jews of Algeria. For further information on the Jews of Tunisia, see *Le Monde Juif*, 15 (January 1949), pp. 10–12; Borgel, *Etoile jaune.*

20. See Alteras, "Holocaust in the Middle East," pp. 101–9.

21. See Gaon and Serels, eds., *Sephardim and the Holocaust*, p. 70.

22. Ibid., pp. 69–70.

Hatred Hurt Them into Poetry

My people you do not know
    in days of old the exodus from ease
scattered them into a thousand nations

My people do not resemble you
    followers of the Covenant
identified with God

My people do not exist
    banished from memory
at the gates of the camps

Henriette Asseo

The Sephardic victims of the Holocaust were, indeed, forgotten at the gates of the camps. Their tragedy at the hands of Nazi Germany remained unknown, and it is only in the voices of the poets and commentators that their experiences are recorded.[1] The concern that dominates all of this material is the fervent, almost pathological need of the survivors and of the authors—those who were in the camps and those who learned from them—to give expression to their inner conflicts. On the one hand, they long to forget the expulsion, dispersion, oppression, and extermination of their brothers and sisters. On the other hand, they feel a contradictory compulsion, as a sacred task, to tell those who were not part of that terrible inferno about the unimaginable crimes, lest the world forgets.

The strong desire to obliterate from one's mind an important, yet horrifying, personal experience was vividly—if silently—conveyed to me in April of 1982 by Lucy Soto from Salonika, Greece, who now lives in Atlanta, Georgia, and by a survivor from Rhodes residing near Tel Aviv, Israel. Their muteness is the result of suffering, many years after the catastrophe, and the lack of a rational way of expressing the horrors they witnessed. Alfred Elkoubi, a native of North Africa and now a resident of Paris, at first expressed his fervent desire to be the messenger of those "cherished ones who perished brutally." Eager to immortalize "the memory of the victims of the death camps," he soon lapsed into silence, for the terrible and painful drama was too dreadful to recall. Yet even though he could not speak, Elkoubi did not betray the annihilated. His silence told the story of the degradation of his Jewish brothers and sisters and the shame of all humanity for being a bystander to this massacre. Those who perished and those who survived spoke through Elkoubi's eyes.

Elie Wiesel, a survivor of Auschwitz and preeminent spokesman of the tragedy, has touched us all. The written word has been his way of speaking on behalf of the Jews who have suffered throughout history, as well as on behalf of all humankind. "Not to transmit an experience is to betray it," he comments.[2] A character, obviously Wiesel himself, states in the *Legends of Our Time:* "The act of writing is for me often nothing more than the secret or conscious desire to carve words on a tombstone: to the memory of a town forever vanished, to the memory of a childhood in exile, to the memory of all those I loved and who, before I could tell them I loved them, went away."[3] In a 1984 visit to the University of South Carolina, Wiesel silently listened to the eloquent introduction by the president of the local chapter of Amnesty International, who recalled the achievements and personal drama of the guest speaker. Suddenly, Wiesel's expression changed drastically, his eyes burned with passion, and his face evidenced the grief and horror he and other Jews had experienced in the extermination camps. No single word, at that or any other moment, could memorialize the tragedy of the Jewish nation. Wiesel's silent witness, his momentary solitude, was overpowering to those of us who escaped the Holocaust and who now give testimony to the loss of close relatives and six million brothers and sisters of the faith.

Not everyone is willing to share their experience of the tragedy with others, as I saw time and again during my conversations with more than one hundred Sephardic survivors. Ruth Beker, a Viennese victim of the Holocaust, writes in "Don't Show Me":

Don't
Don't show me any more pictures.

I don't want to know
about children in horse carts
about men in cattle carts
about women being taken away
about mass goodbyes, unearthly cries. . . .

No. My grandparents were not murdered.
No. My parents were not slaves.
No. My arm has no number. . . .

Don't show me any more.
Don't tell me any more.
Don't.[4]

However, the primary duty of Sephardic writers is not the verbalization of the message but rather the message as a means of retaining their own identity through the remembrance of fallen brothers and sisters. Ben Ruby says, in "Listen My Brother":[5]

I call you my brother
because you are;
of lineage,
of blood,
of faith . . .

It is remembrance, or rather veneration, of the laws, historical happenings, and ancestors that will always identify the Jews with their past, their present, and their future. One cannot divorce history and religion from the Jewish experience, even for those who lost their faith as a result of the horrors that befell them and their families. The message itself is a commitment to one's own survival, that is, to Jewish survival, Jewish unity, and Jewish collective destiny. For Jews, life is the cultivation of the traditions of their forebears and the zeal to share these customs with their children and the world at large—for this is the task of Israel. The hope for an emancipated and dignified future, bonded with its past, is affirmed by Ben Ruby as he reaches out for his dead brother:

Stay.
I shall spend with you
this chill night . . .
But tomorrow,
oh, tomorrow!
A bright sun
will shine on your face,
and hand in hand,
with a firm step,
we shall walk together, my brother,
—shall we?—
on the road
of human dignity
and liberty.

("Listen My Brother")

Chelomo Reuven, in a poem entitled "Yom Hachoa" and composed in memory of his mother and his dear ones who disappeared in Auschwitz, first recounts the terrible drama that plagued his people and tells of his everlasting personal torment:

> Incurable is the wound because great is the tragedy;
> the tears have dried and the pain does not cease.
> The day passes, the night comes, and a new day dawns
> without suppressing my moans, without my accepting my
> misfortune.

He suffers as he retraces the path of the Salonikan people through the vast necropolis of the death camps, their unending march to the gas chamber, and their final journey as a heavy gray cloud rising through the chimneys with the stench of death. The pain is excruciating for the poet, who realizes that the tragedy took place while the whole world was present at the macabre spectacle and did nothing.

Still, in the true spirit of his ancestors and faithful to his Jewish upbringing, Reuven cannot end "Yom Hachoa" in total despair. He finds in the death of the "beloved souls" the strength to go on living and a new hope in the restoration of the Promised Land:

> But over the death camps and from that gray cloud
> grew the delicate flower of our liberation;
> and over the beloved bones and mountains of ash,
> at the cost of new blood, our nation was restored.
>
> Rest, beloved souls, from your last sleep.
> You have fallen. With your death, evil seemed to have conquered,
> but with your last breath, you have given life to our genius
> and our lips murmur: "Yitgadal veyitkadash."

The lips of the poet murmur the Kaddish, the ancient mourner's prayer recited by Israel as a permanent testimony to the dead and to glorify and sanctify God's great name in spite of His silence during the tribulations inflicted on His people. It is the spirit expressed in the Kaddish that links the past with the present and the future and that underscores the unity of the Jews. "If not all victims were Jews, all Jews were victims," points out Elie Wiesel in *The Dimensions of the Holocaust*. Ben Ruby, Reuven, and a great number of the poets of Sepharad share that sentiment.

Henriette Asseo, in "My People," states that ever since the Exodus from the Holy Land, the descendants of the Hebrews, estranged from other nations, have not only remained faithful to the Covenant but have continued their identification with Adonai. She claims that "My people do not exist / banished from memory / at the gates of the camps." But this is not so, for the silence of others did not stifle the voice of the Sephardic poets, nor hold back the chisel of the sculptor, nor the brush of the painter. The voices of the dead cry out, accuse, and demand through Reuven's "Salonika" that their story be told:

"Where is the artist who will paint the tragedy?
Where is the poet who will mourn us?"
The day begins, night falls, and a new day dawns,
And the world still waits for that voice,

The voice that will bemoan our fate and will demand
Vengeance for the crime that has no expiation;
That voice that, in its accounts, would include all the anxiety
And affliction that befell the martyred people of Israel.

The same voices scattered in the mountains of Ponar (Ponary), in the graves of Belsen, Dachau, and Estonia, and in many, many other killing centers where the Jews were sent to die, refuse to let the Sephardic poet Esther Morguez Algrante rest. The victims persistently question the motives for their tragic fate:

My soul turns toward the graves of the dead,
Whence I hear the voices asking me:
"Why were we mistreated, destroyed?"
"Why were we burned?" they cry out to me in distress.

("In Memory of the Warsaw Ghetto")

Remembrance of and vindication for the children of Israel who were interned in Auschwitz were also promised by a group of young women from Rhodes while they awaited their own fate. Their thoughts were with those in the camps and with their dear ones far away. They implored the silent God to answer their call for liberation and return them to their homes:

O Great God! Answer, even You.
We do not want to remain here any longer.
We promise with sure and certain faith
One day to avenge our dear ones.

("Here in This Land")

In "My Thoughts on the Warsaw Ghetto," Morguez Algrante paints a shattering image of intense pain and perplexing thoughts, a state of mind that is always present but becomes more severe on Yom Hachoa, the day set aside to commemorate the eventful happenings:

Each year on that same day
My thoughts grant me no rest.
Unfailingly they present themselves
Before my eyes in a ghastly tableau.

Horrifying figures come suddenly
Stubbornly to disturb my sleep
Of that terrifying Nazi-contrived agony
For my brothers killed with such brutality.

She cannot forget her dead brothers and sisters and their cry for justice. Imploring the heavens to join in the remembrance for those who never lost their faith, believed in the One God, and honored with dignity His Law, she is one of several Sephardic poets to answer the call of Reuven's questioners. The eyes of six million innocent martyrs are fixed on her and will not permit her to forget them.

Thus ... Every single year I will remember
My tortured and burned brothers.
With writings and elegies I will lament them,
For in my heart they remain forever engraved.

Yehuda Haim Perahia, a native of Salonika who was hidden during the last years of the war by a Greek Orthodox family, feels the excruciating pain when he visualizes "the beloved children of persecuted Israel" in wretched captivity and the devastation of his native city, once the glory of Israel in the Diaspora. Beaten, his head bowed, he could not resign himself to the situation, for the misfortunes of his people were many and touched him deeply throughout his life. As his two close friends Esther Morguez Algrante and Chelomo Reuven have done in their poetry, he also expresses his anguish and desperation in "After the Catastrophe in Salonika," written on August 8, 1945:

I see corteges of human beings, en masse, herded into wagons
Of animals, frozen, closed, and sealed like melons,
Brought to the funereal and cursed places of execution,
The aged and sick condemned on the spot.

Afterward also the young, sent to the baths to wash,
Asphyxiated all together, unable ever to rise again,
Then thrown, pushed into the sinister and dreadful crematoria;
There vanished from my people a great number of Jews!

A tragedy such as this has never happened before in the world!
At the thought of this, my vision darkens at once.
My tears fall; my cry is that of a decent man.
I run away quickly, hiding my pain within myself.

In Tel Aviv in 1982, Leon Reuven Cohen, one of 135 Greek Jews who were assigned to the gas chambers, described for me the gruesome masses of corpses piled in large rooms awaiting cremation after the seemingly endless files of the living were killed by a few pellets of Zyklon B. Henriette Asseo's "Ecological Attila," written in the 1980s, interprets faithfully a similar ghastly scene:

On my people
on the corpses of my people
on the pieces of the corpses of my people
on the chunks of the corpses of my people
on the piles of the chunks of the corpses of my people
on the piles of the pieces of the corpses of my people
on the heaps of the corpses of my people
in Maidanek and Auschwitz
in Birkenau and Treblinka
only green
          grass.

The frightening cattle cars, the endless files, the dying screams in the gas chambers, the burning fires in the open pits and crematoria, and the chimneys robbing the final resting place of the dead will forever remain engraved in the survivors' memories. No longer will the Jews be mute. They will transmit through literary compositions, paintings, and other artistic means the message of the Holocaust in order to prevent the occurrence of more such catastrophes for Jews and Gentiles alike. Their own historical past has imprinted in their minds that such acts are not foreign to any generation. It is a fear that has been expressed time and again by Jewish writers, such as the Salonikan-born Itzhak Ben Ruby, in *El sekreto del mudo* (The secret of the mute).[6] The epigraph states, ". . . In 1945 the world did not do everything possible to destroy radically the monstrous Hitlerian serpent. The danger of someday seeing it wake up from its drowsiness weighs heavily on all humanity."

Violette Fintz, a survivor of Auschwitz and today one of the most ardent messengers for all the victims, has vowed to keep alive their memory. Her mission, which entails neither hatred nor punishment for the executioners, "is to tell the story and to remind the world of man's inhumanity to his fellow men." When I interviewed Violette Fintz in 1984 in Brussels—while she was visiting from South Africa—I did not detect any anger or bitterness but a cry, a plea, that this tragedy should never be repeated. "That it happened once, unbelievable as it seems, means it could happen again. Hitler made it possible for anyone. Neither Jew nor any group on earth can feel safe from that crime in the future."[7] Holocaust scholar Yehuda Bauer points to the readiness of individuals to perpetrate the most appalling injustices, even mass murder, under certain circumstances. He warns us that because the instruments of slaughter are becoming more deadly, the methods of bureaucratic control more efficient, and the hatred of minorities more entrenched, the danger of genocide is actually growing.[8]

Through their writings the Sephardic poets hope to warn humanity of the vivid possibility of its own debasement, its own disintegration, its own total destruction. But their primary purpose in telling the truth of the turbulent days is to eulogize the martyrs, to immortalize the suffering of the survivors, and to try to absolve themselves of the personal accusations that haunt them for not sharing the fate of their people in the ghettos and camps. This desire and duty to be the voice of the annihilated community account for the authors' sense of alienation and their feelings of personal guilt. Esther Morgues Algrante writes:

> Immediately my trial begins thus,
> My conscience questions me incessantly:
> "Well, now, speak, answer. Why are you still alive,
> When six million lost their lives?"
>
> ("My Thoughts on the Warsaw Ghetto")

Wherever he walked on a visit to his native Salonika after the Holocaust, Chelomo Reuven saw in the empty streets countless old people, relatives, friends, and the faces of thousands of innocent children killed without any hesitation. Their excruciating laments reached his ears and would not let him rest:

> "Man! Where were you?" they ask. "Tell us:
> When we were all arrested in this same city,

When we were deported, when the Sonderkommandos
Suffocated our old and young in the gas?

"Tell us: where were you when, feeble and exhausted,
Swollen by hunger, dried with thirst,
We were hurled into the ovens and thus burned,
And the executioners slaughtered with no mercy?"

("Salonika")

He weeps at the thought that he was safe in Palestine during the long years of World War II, while his relatives, his friends, and his coreligionists agonized and died a terrible death solely for being born Jews. As he explained to me in 1982 in Tel Aviv: "The terrible drama of the death camps will forever torment my memory. The thought of not being able to help and to soothe the pain of my dear ones in their hour of need will remain forever a scar in my heart."

To alleviate their "innocent" guilt, the living must submit to the catharsis of suffering:

God sternly charges me to feel remorse:
"Go into mourning, do penance, lament,
Grieve for this disaster, for this wickedness,
For this slaughter unique in history."

So writes Morguez Algrante in "My Thoughts on the Warsaw Ghetto," from the safety of her native Turkey. Yehuda Perahia expresses the same anguish in "Tisha Beav 5704." Hidden in Greece, protected by his faithful servant, Anastasia, the poet compares the destruction of the Temple to the extermination of his people Israel in the twentieth century. His pain was intensified upon seeing himself shielded by his Creator, who hid him from the Bulgarians, Germans, Greeks, and Italians. He rebelled against the same Eternal God for not spreading His hand over all Jewry and in his solitude wished to be dead. In total pessimism Perahia thought of destroying everything. His preoccupation turned him away from the salvation of humankind, from all the necessities of life, and from the normal functioning of nature and the universe. As long as his people suffered, life was meaningless:

And as long as Samael and Asmodeus laugh at our suffering,
And as long as Matatron and the Angels do nothing but cry,
What do I care, Holy God, in view of the condition of my people,
An almost eternal situation, the worst on all the Earth,
Where never reigned and never shall reign but the right of the
     strong,
What do I care, Eternal God, whether I live or die?

The self-guilt and mental anguish of those condemned to live, while family and friends were singled out to die, often gave rise to envy for the dead and to personal sacrifice: the giving of one's life to spare another's. For Hanna Senech, a Hungarian Jewish heroine who fought with the Resistance, as well as for many unknown martyrs in the camps, there was no greater sacrifice than to face willingly the hangman's noose, the firing squad, or the sting of gas so that others might survive:

> Blessed is the heart with strength to stop
>   its beating for honor's sake.
> Blessed is the match that is consumed
>   in kindling flame.[9]

The poets of Sepharad cry for not having been able to give themselves for those who suffered, for not being part of the tragedy. They are determined to give voice to the victims, to become witnesses of the witnesses, by listening to the survivors and feeling the anguish of their own families and friends. Arthur A. Cohen declares: "The task of this literature was neither to astonish nor to amaze, neither to exalt nor humiliate, but to provide a vivifying witness to the flesh of the dead. . . ."[10] Like Elie Wiesel, the Sephardic poets realize that "bearing witness does have its own life and function. . . . The witness re-establishes human continuity, speaking for the dead and to the living, preserving the past in order to guard the future." This is a complicated process, darkly empowered, which Ellen Fine sums up brilliantly by restating Wiesel's notion that to listen to the witness is to become a witness.[11] In the words of Jacques Taraboulos of Jerusalem, to be a witness not only gives life and identity to the survivor but also calms the feelings of guilt, despair, and self-accusation of those who were not part of the Holocaust. Witnessing rekindles the hope for a better future for all humankind.

Still, the conflicting voices of hope and despair, of faith and doubt, and the final realization that no rational explanation ever was (indeed, could be) given for the Holocaust—no more than that which was given for the persecutions of the Jews by the Assyrians, Babylonians, Egyptians, Romans, Spaniards, Russians, and other oppressors through the ages—have given rise to the questioning of the validity of the Covenant between God and Israel. Many generations of Jews have felt forsaken by God and have questioned His actions. The patriarchs, Moses, Job, the prophets, all have, time and again, put the Lord to the test for what He did to His people or for staying silent in their hour of need. So, too, the modern Sephardic poets have questioned what unkind fate has stricken Israel ever since the days of Mount Moriah when Abraham was ordered by Adonai to offer his son, Isaac, as a burnt offering—the supreme act of faith, in what the *Encyclopaedia Judaica* calls "the first test in a series of covenants between God and Israel." The Sephardic survivors and poets are aware that the trials of faith continued during the Holocaust and persist to this day in the Soviet Union, in Poland—the cradle of the killing centers of Chelmo, Sobibor, Treblinka, Maidanek, Auschwitz, Birkenau—in Arab countries, and to a lesser degree in Western nations where anti-Semitism is still alive.

While some Jewish writers have challenged the existence of God and have rejected Him for not fulfilling the Divine Promise, the Sephardic poets, with very few exceptions, have no doubt of God's greatness and of His presence in the daily activities of His people. Whether He is a silent God, whether He chooses to hide from His people, He is still the Savior, the one to whom His people turn in their hour of need. Nevertheless, the Sephardic poets attempt to justify His "impersonality" and "incomprehensible" silence while millions of Jews were fed into the fires. Some have found that God was very near to them in the camps and that He had specific purposes in His actions. Alfred Elkoubi informed me that the tragedy was a detour in his life and, because of it, his outlook on humanity has changed. More important, because of the Holocaust he found a mate, who gave him children dedicated to the service of God, Israel, and humanity. God had challenged his faith—and that of many, he was quick to say—and ever since that moment he has felt a sense of obligation to maintain the beliefs of his ancestors: "To forget my religion, that I was a Jew, is to dishonor my dead relatives and to honor that monster Hitler. I believe more and I will believe until my dying days. It is my mission." This answer, given to me by a survivor who had lost his entire family in Auschwitz, typifies what Reeve Robert Brenner calls a "Holocaust Mitzvah."[12]

The religious belief of some of the surviving Sephardim may have been shaken during the Holocaust, and their daily practice decreased immediately after the tragedy, yet very few gave up their observance. Like many of their Ashkenazic brothers and sisters, they prayed in the camps, fasted on Yom Kippur, kept the Sabbath holy, and uttered the Kaddish and the Shema on their death march, not as an act of defiance but of faith. In spite of this, the Sephardic poet does not preclude the intellectual sounding out of God's role and the excruciating question "Why?" The "silent," "eclipsed," or "hidden" God does not keep Yehuda Perahia from believing that his Maker is reachable. Because of his religious background in Salonika, a city of thirty synagogues headed by pious rabbis, and his direct descent from Joseph ben Matatia Flavius (Flavius Josephus), Perahia believes in the omnipotence of a God who will redeem His people Israel. However, in "Hanukah 5704," following the tradition of Judaism, he cries out:

> How long, compassionate God, will I go on lamenting?
> How long the tribulations of my people will I suffer?
> How long will my head be a cistern of water
> And my eyes running springs of bitter tears?

The pain becomes unbearable and Perahia agonizes upon hearing that the war continues, that innocent beings from among his unfortunate people, the nation God chose, are dying. In desperation he reminds the Lord,

> And nevertheless, You had promised our ancestors,
> Even in the land of their enemies under Heaven:
> "I will be merciful unto them, my children, and I shall not destroy them;
> In their hours of oppression I shall come to them and redeem them."

("The Third Cry in Anguish in Salonika")

Esther Morguez Algrante, the daughter of a rabbi, suffers for the six million Jews whose fixed eyes stare at her and torment her. God charges her, "Go into mourning, do penance, lament," yet He is indifferent to the agony of those who never lost faith in Him and who believed in His Law. In "My Thoughts on the Warsaw Ghetto," Morguez Algrante cries out:

> O God! How could You permit such a catastrophe?
> How could You grant power to a monster?
> O God! I implore You to punish cruelly
> The one who did this to Your Chosen.

Enrique Saporta y Beja, a Sephardi who was able to escape the Holocaust by obtaining a Spanish passport, questions what became of the deported.[13] His answers only recapitulate their suffering and final annihilation, and his poem is not complete until he asks God the reason for His indifference. In the end, Saporta affirms the faith of the Jews in God even though they have been the target of many persecutions:

—God in Heaven, God of goodness,
  How have You allowed these cruelties?
  How have You not prevented
  The Final Solution
  And have allowed the mowing down
  Of so many Jewish men and women?

—But even though wounded in many places,
  We have not lost faith in You.

("What Has Become of Them? Questions with Replies")

The indictments against God multiply. As in Elie Wiesel's *Ani Maamim*, the Sephardic Jew "raises many of the traditional Jewish strategies for defending the plausibility structure of the theodicy [and] dismisses each of them."[14] There is an angelic voice in Wiesel's cantata that defends God when He is attacked by the patriarchs for His actions against the Jews, and God is finally moved by and weeps for His people's declarations of faith in the midst of their suffering. But on two occasions in the poems of the Sephardim God reacts more readily to the outcry of His people: when the mothers of Israel lament the tragedy that has befallen their children (Perahia's "Vision"); and when the soul of a child, together with the soul of the Torah, ascends to Heaven and, in a mystic union, merges with God.

The Sephardic poet notices that while God is silent, even some of the torturers cry at the sight of the tragedy and their hearts burst into wails and moanings. Nature is despondent; the birds do not sing and the cocks sleep rather than announce the coming of a new dawn; the air is filled with the lugubrious sound of the death of the innocent. In vain the poets address God, asking His mercy. In despair they implore the angels to intervene, as in the days of old when Isaac was to be sacrificed:

Heavens. Angels. Cry out for them, I pray,
The never-to-be-forgotten martyrs of the Jewish nation.
Recite the Kaddish aloud and weep
For these souls whom Death brought us to mourn.

(Morguez Algrante, "My Thoughts on the Warsaw Ghetto")

The prophets, beside themselves, ask for deliverance. The angels, in their grief, indict God for ordering the death sentence.

"You, Lord, ordained this," said the good Matatron.
Elijah the Prophet, running to and fro, asked if there were any
    rescue.
The angels, headed by Raphael and Michael, did not speak;
Rather they all read psalms, shed tears, and wailed.

(Perahia, "A Tragedy")

The Lord, unmoved, remains silent, a mere spectator to the agony
of those who would perish in the fires. He chooses not to save the
nation that served Him "in centuries of gold / in centuries of dark-
ness." Even the *Malahe a sharet* (the angels who serve Him), dejected
by their failure, rend their wings and descend from the heavens to
accompany the martyrs. They, too, deliver themselves into the burn-
ing fires. "And the Ancient of Days / will remain silent," says Avner
Perets in "Cast into the Fire."

In spite of the queries arising from the living and the dead, and
now abandoned by His angels, God persists in His silence. The poets,
in despair, accuse their Maker of hiding His face and permitting such
atrocities to occur. They remind God of His responsibility, of His
moral obligations toward His people—that He chose to be the Lord,
the God, to bring them out of the land of Egypt, out of the house of
bondage (Exodus 20:2). They insist that God initiated the Covenant
with the Jews on Mount Moriah and finalized it in Sinai by giving
them the Torah. Perahia, referring to the agony of the time, charges
God with being insensitive to the long suffering of His people:

You made a covenant with us to serve You.
You become angry because we do not obey and from Your ways we
    deviate.
But this covenant—You made it with Your people,
And for that reason, You should show Yourself always more
    indulgent.

....

God of the Universe! Is it that we wanted to be born Jews,
When fate decided our coming into the world?
You know it well: Is it that we wanted to be born?
No one, in any way or manner, asked for our advice.

("In the Agony of Time")

God remains silent.

The obligations He demands from His people are awesome, and
God's chosen servants can no longer endure the calamities that have

befallen them for more than two thousand years. Besides, a covenant is an alliance and, as such, requires reciprocity from both partners; if one's duties are not fulfilled, the partnership is no longer valid. Thus, the Sephardic poets question God's intent in choosing the Jews. They cry out in despair, but with no malice toward others, asking Him to sanctify other peoples. In one of three stanzas of an anonymous poem I located in Israel, the poet implores,

> It is time You take pity on him
> And praise other nations;
> Their virtues You should laud
> And for the wretched Jew no more aversions.

Perahia, a faithful servant of Adonai, cannot understand why the Jews are uprooted and destroyed "all together and completely" for their sins, while other peoples are made to suffer only for their own misdeeds. He asks God to grant the Jew a divorce from a marriage contracted in Heaven:

> You have brought us to the point of telling You in spite of ourselves
> That we are weary of being Your pitiful children.
> Short of being "Mamhelet coanim ve goy kadosh,"[15] and we cry,
> Take other peoples and sanctify them in our stead.

("In the Agony of Time")

He knows that Israel was chosen by the Lord from among all nations for a definite purpose—that is, to glorify the name of Adonai, to be the missionary of the Law, and to keep His Sabbath holy. He also knows that God has chosen to reveal His presence only through His people and that He can only do so as long as they exist. Perahia affirms that "God and the Jews are inseparable," and so he warns Him:

> O Holy God! Who will now read the abandoned Torah?
> Here there were many groups who read it and lived by it.
> Who will keep the Sabbath, the great day of rest?
> How can You be present as a spectator of this tragedy?

("The Third Cry in Anguish in Salonika")

The prayers, the accusations, the admonitions, all go unanswered. When there is no hope for redemption, Perahia (in the poem cited above, written in 1943), already fearful that he has blasphemed, cries out, yet again, asking God to keep the promise He made to Israel:

Lord of the Universe, Lord of the Universe! If you were a man
I would have brought You to judgment even in Your holy name!
But You are not a man and I blaspheme. And what can I do
But cry endlessly, since I cannot conceive
That You should thus have us obliterated by our oppressors.
Keep Your promise and send us our saviors quickly.[16]

When, in 1945, he can no longer endure the painful end to which
the Eternal God has brought his people, when he cannot understand
why he was left as a living testimony to the prophecies of the Torah
while others of his faith were being destroyed, he considers his own
death:

Of all your utterances, great Prophet Isaiah,
And of all your soothings, O Jeremiah, I only see promises.
My dark pessimism presses me to blaspheme;
Bitter irony that causes me to think of destroying everything:

("Tisha Beav 5704")

The long quarrel with God would continue and the disaster of
the Holocaust would give rise to denunciations of His acts and to
threats that the Covenant was no longer operative. There would be
countless justifications for blasphemy, but the poets could not bring
themselves to commit such an act. Even in their outrage and their
anguish they would insist on believing in God and in praising His
holy name. No deed of Adonai, however terrible, would make the
Jews renounce their faith and their hope in Him. To the incessant
question "Where is God?" many in the camps concluded either that
He was no longer present in history or that His presence was eclipsed;
or, most frightening to some, that He was still alive. When asked,
"Andi esta el Dio?" (Where is God?), a Sephardic inmate in Ausch-
witz replied to Mr. Kamhi, a fellow Greek Jew: "No saves? Si fue
de vakasion. Aki azi mucho frio i esta mizeravle" (Don't you know?
He went on vacation. It is too cold and miserable here).

Several poems and anecdotes have surfaced from those who
miraculously escaped the concentration camps and from their core-
ligionists who still believed in the presence of God, though a silent
God untouched by the prayers of the innocent and especially by the
suffering of the faithful, the pious, and the blameless children. One
man, now living in Israel, told me that when he failed to find God
in his daily prayers, he exclaimed to one of his countrymen, "Si el
Dio siente mis orasiones, desgrasiado yo" (If the Lord hears my

prayer, poor me). In a recent conversation, a pious Sephardic survivor yielded a simple, yet profound, response when I questioned him about his faith during his ordeal in Auschwitz and other concentration camps: "Rogi i rogi i rogi. Bendicho sea el nombri del Dio, ma El nunka respondio, nunka . . . , nunka . . . , nunka . . ." (I prayed and I prayed and I prayed. Blessed be the name of the Lord, but He never answered, never . . . , never . . . , never . . .).

The arrival of the trains, crammed with thousands of Jews who thought they were being repatriated, gave rise to the following anecdote, told to me by Mr. Leon Cohen, who heard it from a fellow Salonikan Jew:

> An old man from back home always sat in the camp and thanked God for His mercy and goodness toward His people. Every day he would see the trains arrive packed with people. In a pious manner, he would thank the Lord for increasing the lot. He would say: "Lord of the Universe, You always fulfilled Your promise to have us multiply, and here we are multiplying by the day and by the hour, even our dead are multiplying. Yes, Lord, our prayers are also multiplying, even Your absence is multiplying. O Lord! Why are You not here with us?"[17]

Understandably, world catastrophes do affect religious beliefs, especially for the long-persecuted Jews who have endured all the unbearable calamities since being singled out by the God of the patriarchs. Yet, in spite of the deeds perpetrated against them throughout history and their excruciating bewilderment and indictment of God's insensibility to their tragedies, culminating with the Holocaust, they, as their forebears for four millennia, have maintained their unique relationship with God, the source of their pride and being. It is the Jewish faith in the Desert God that has kept Israel united, a fact that even many surviving unbelievers cannot refute. Of course, it is obvious that faith would be destroyed should all Jews be annihilated. However, three rhetorical questions must inevitably be asked—the same three that secular Jews as well as religious Jews have pondered after each national calamity: Can Israel reject its Covenant with God and survive? Can Israel survive as other nations do once it is divorced from its ethnic heritage and religious laws, thus eradicating the source of anti-Semitism? Can the God of Sinai remain silent in the face of such atrocities and still survive in the hearts and minds of the Chosen?

The answer to these questions perhaps lies in an anecdote told by Elie Wiesel, who heard it while interned in a camp whose name he does not mention: "Once, three learned Jews who were heads of academies, decided to put God on trial for what He had done to His Chosen People. Evening after evening, sitting on the beds, the men argued the case gravely because they knew that their verdict would become widely known. After great discussion they brought in the verdict: 'Guilty.' Intuitively, the response of the Head of the Tribunal was: 'And now, let's go and pray.' "[18] A similar story was reported by a Sephardic Jew:

> A young man, tired of the endless horrors that he and his people endured day in and day out at the hands of human beasts, questioned God's part in the crimes and His failing to bring justice to the camps and carry out His duties to His people: "Tio," he would say. "Why all the prayers? Why recite the Kaddish for the dead. Will God protect them more in heaven than He does on earth?"
>
> The old man would sit quietly and listen attentively. Not having any answers that would satisfy the young man or himself, he would agree that God was insensitive and cruel at times. "These questions have to be considered," he would say, "but, first let us ask God for guidance."[19]

In 1942, when the oppression had barely begun in Greece, Yehuda Perahia responded to a friend in Kavalla:

> Friend, you ask me why they hounded us to death,
> Are we such sinners to merit this fate?
> Why did God take us to be His chosen people
> And for that reason bear endless tortures and sufferings?

Finding no satisfactory answers, he first accused God, then he resigned himself to his fate and, like Job, realized that the questions were too difficult:

> What you ask cannot be resolved in a few words;
> Many, there are so very many, basic and convincing answers to give.
> I do not possess complete and absolute competence to clarify them.
> In all the workings of the universe I see the hand of Providence.
>
> To this mighty and invisible power everything is subjected;
> The mover of the world and of living men's destinies.
> Not a single thing or movement can escape His attention;
> His eye penetrates everything, following the world's rotation.

Indeed, Perahia came to realize that, regardless of our intellect, we cannot penetrate the depths of the unknown:

> To Him alone belong all secrets.
> He answers to none. But through signs

He showed us the way to perfect virtue,
Leaving us free to follow Him or take the road to perdition.

("A Reply")

Perahia, like other Sephardic poets, knows that the prophets Amos, Hosea, Isaiah, Micah, Zephaniah, Nahum, Jeremiah, and all other speakers for God have preached to the Israelites that "Yahweh was not a placable local jinn, but the just Lord of Heaven and Earth."[20] One way to please Him is to keep His commandments, not to rob the poor, oppress the weak, pervert justice, or condone wickedness. "They must cleanse themselves of lust and hatefulness, and be decent, kindly, pure. If they refused, then despite the fact that they were Yahweh's 'chosen people,' indeed just because of it, they would be destroyed—even as Israel had been destroyed."[21] Perahia thus suggests in "A Reply" that Israel examine itself:

As Jews we have many duties to perform and fullfil.
Is it not that we strayed from them instead of approaching them?
Is our conscience cleared of our sins?
Is it that we have nothing to reproach ourselves for before
    Providence?

The children of Israel must mend their ways and repent while there is time. They must accept God's punishment for their sins and keep the Law given to them, for it is their only means of survival and unity. In Sinai, God gave the Jews free will. He gave them the power to reason, to choose freedom and peace within their tradition, or to choose despair and persecution by assimilating with the peoples of other nations and adopting their godless ways. Abraham Joshua Heschel maintains that "God will return to us when we shall be willing to let Him in. . . . There is a divine dream. . . . It is a dream of a world, rid of evil by the grace of God as well as by the efforts of man. . . . God is waiting to redeem the world. We should not spend our life hunting for trivial satisfactions while God is waiting constantly and keenly for our effort and devotion."[22] The poets of Sepharad are in total agreement.

In a long poem entitled "Vision," written on the eve of Yom Kippur 5704 (September 1944), Perahia inserted fifteen stanzas which he later crossed out with a red marker, noting that they were of a personal nature. It is only by permission of his family and of the leaders of the community that I refer to them here. In these verses God chides the Salonikan Jewry—symbolic of all Jewish communities—for abandoning the Law and the traditions of their forebears. He accuses the people of deserting their religion, of profaning the Sabbath, and of violating the Commandments. God declares that their conduct was based on hypocrisy and lies, and He deplores that the ways of the past—the unity of the family, respect for one's parents and religious leaders, the giving of alms, the protection of widows and orphans—were all desecrated. Unlike the Greek Orthodox mothers' love for their children and for "instructing them about their idols," the Jewish mothers are singled out for raising their offspring apart from "the praised religion" and for encouraging assimilation to "alien evil customs."

Perahia writes that the silence of God was the result of His long suffering caused by the sins of Israel. In His solitude, He awaited the return of His people and agonized about the destruction of His communities at the hands of other nations. He, too, felt abandoned and dejected. More than once He was eager to intervene on behalf of His people, who never relinquished their transgressions and thus suffered for their sins. He could hear their groans and, as a father, could not bear to see them die without Himself crying; as a mother, He could not witness the tortures brought upon His children without Himself lamenting. The violations of the Law multiplied and the people were on the road to total perdition:

> But the cup filled and it ran overabundantly!
> My whole heart trembled, my soul felt sadness.
> It was I who took the decision before the weeping of the Angels.
> The earth shook, the Heavens filled with Seraphim.
> . . . .
>
> Woe is Me for I wish to justify myself!
> I wonder how to blame Myself for your evil deeds.
> You personally wanted your downfall;
> With other peoples you wanted freely to assimilate.
>
> ("Vision")

Failing to reproach Himself, Perahia says, God, in His infinite love, resolved to punish the people in order to prevent their own total destruction:

> Then, my rage burst! I could not give you the pleasure
> Of destroying yourselves and thus disappear.
> All at once, I struck you mortally and I did away with you
> Without giving you the time to think so as not to suffer.
>
> ("Vision")

But the suffering of the children infuriated the mothers of Israel—Sarah, Leah, Rachel, and Rebecca. Like roaring lionesses they leapt against their Maker, whom they had always adored. Where the angels had failed, the formidable wails of the matriarchs, as did the testimony of faith by the Jews in Wiesel's *Ani Maamin*, profoundly moved God, who now feared for the lives of His chosen people. The lamentations of the mothers swiftly appeased His rage and caused Him to hide many from the deportations. It also stirred Him to send Michael to save Israel and Raphael to soothe and sustain those in captivity.

Jacques Taraboulos, in "The Neila" (1945), presents a great God of love, yet a God who is about to inscribe in the Book of Life and Death the fate of each individual Jew according to merit. However, at the most crucial hour of Yom Kippur, while the Ark is wide open, the voice and soul of a child, in unison with the Torah, ascend to Heaven and pray for the victims of the Holocaust and for the souls of the other children of Israel, as well as for those of all creation who have not reached God. The Eternal One grows sad for the suffering of His people and for the admission of the child and the Torah that "the sin is in man" and that forgiveness is in the Lord. When the Torah, which is in God and is God, unites the soul of the child with that of the Lord in a mystic bond, a touched God does not close the Book of Life and Death at the prescribed hour. The poet informed me in an interview in Jerusalem in 1982 that the all-merciful God renounces His absolute justice and, as a forgiving and loving father, controls His anger and restrains Himself rather than pronounce the verdict due.

Abraham Joshua Heschel finds a God who "will return to us when we shall be willing to let Him in . . . into every facet of our life."[23] The God of the Sephardic poets exonerates the people of Israel even before they atone for their sins; He does not wait for the sinners to find their way to Him. Adonai, in lifting the burden of punishment from the Jews, warns the poet Perahia, in "Vision," that Israel must adhere to the Covenant and observe the Law and traditions:

Live now and be more fortunate than those in previous years.
But, return, return to the good traditions of long ago,
Follow the precepts of the Torah and you shall be blessed;
You will know true joy with beautiful results.

Like the innocent child in Taraboulos's "The Neila," Perahia repeatedly confesses that we are sinners but reminds God that we are

His children, created in His image, and should be saved. He tells the Almighty that the Jews are at the mercy of countless enemies whose blood is replete with dangerous instincts, whose hearts lack "love, compassion, peace, and goodness," and who know no justice. For that reason Perahia insists that God should have given us a compassionate nature:

> . . . man is the most ferocious of all animals;
> The strong attacks the weak in the most criminal ways.
> And what can one say of us, a few defenseless people,
> From whom cruel and perverse enemies take away all strength.

("In the Agony of Time")

In "The Second Cry in Anguish," Perahia tries again to move God, invoking the salvation and preservation of the Jewish people. He presents the terrible state in which the Chosen have found themselves:

> Oh! The enemy struck suddenly at the heart of my people.
> He plundered, robbed, committed crimes without regard for Heaven.
> The children do not find milk in the breasts of their mothers.
> The tears of the young fall with those of their parents.

Of course, this reasoning can stand only as long as one ignores the existence of free will, which God bestowed upon humankind at the Creation. Without it, the Creator, being the prime mover, is responsible for historical happenings and we are nothing but automatons. Perahia says that the individual was created free to choose and act and, as a partner with God, must strive to perfect the world, but this must be done within limits and without disregarding morality. Ultimately, he points to human weakness and wickedness as the source of the Jewish problem. A great number of inmates in the camps did question the silence of God and suffered because of His perceived absence. Yet the physical annihilation, the daily tortures in the death factories, the endless marches, the total dehumanization, these were the works of people; they were not metaphysical in origin.

The Sephardic poets have no doubt that the insanity of the Holocaust cannot be the sole responsibility of God. Still, it is their fervent belief that the Lord must be made to answer for the world He created. One cannot formulate acceptable solutions to God's seeming participation in the slaughter since the philosophical bases for the discussion are themselves speculative. Besides, believers will ultimately tend to affirm their trust in God, while agnostics will continue their search or give up in despair, and atheists will deny the existence of God. None will have grounds for such a trial.

A concern of these poets is the position of the Christian world toward the Jewish nation, particularly during the Holocaust. Perahia, in "The Third Cry in Anguish in Salonika," recounts the innumerable burnings of places of worship, beginning with the Temple in Jerusalem, the degradation of God's Law, and the destruction of His people:

> When criminal hands burned the Beth Amigdash,
> The High Priests threw the keys to Heaven to deliver them.
> Here, it is the strangers who tore in mockery Your holy Law,
> Taking away to death all the followers of Your faith!

Hizkia M. Franco, in "The Deportation," asks St. Paul what he thinks of "this monstrous crime" executed by his followers in Auschwitz:

> Fathers, mothers, children,
> They crushed with no pity.
> Hard were the tortures
> For all sexes and ages.
>
> They smothered tender children
> With no emotion or heart.
> From the wax of these lilies
> They produced, alas! their good soap.

St. Paul, like the apostles and the great majority of bishops, will always remain silent, will not intervene. For them there is no forgiveness for the Jew, no clemency.[24]

The Christian ideals of love, grace, forgiveness, caring for and suffering with one's fellow humans did not apply to the Jews:

> The enemy who, from time immemorial, was watching to harm
> Israel
> Saw with a joyful heart the Jew sigh.
> Like savage beasts they all threw themselves on the spoils;
> ....
> What satisfaction, O Heavenly God, these evildoers felt—
> Throwing themselves like hungry lions on the prey they devoured!
>
> ("The Second Cry in Anguish")

There was no end to the suffering. In the 1940s, office workers watched from windows and balconies as German soldiers attended with glee and mockery the gathering and compulsory physical drills of the Jews of Salonika, ironically held in Freedom Square. Their laughter increased in proportion to the agony of those in custody who were forced to do excruciating calisthenics and were whipped at the whim of the guards for infractions of the command or for the mere pleasure of those in attendance. Such scenes were not limited to Salonika but occurred routinely in occupied lands, where the Nazis and their cohorts committed unspeakable crimes against miserable and wretched human beings whose only sin was to be of Jewish ancestry.

For Jacques Taraboulos, Christians have forgotten what their forebears endured in the arenas of Rome, where they became prey to beasts and adversaries of gladiators, all for the entertainment of leaders and plebeians. Instead of showing mercy to their neighbors, as preached by Christ their Saviour, they were so consumed by hate that they reveled in the persecutions and tortures. He shares the opinion of Max Bueno de Mesquita, a Sephardic painter of the Holocaust and an inmate of Auschwitz who saw his family perish and his life shattered. De Mesquita stated that the love of Christ's children was short-lived and their abomination for others was exhibited early in their history. Taraboulos sees in the sages and leaders of Christianity—in those who could have put an end to the slaughter in the streets, cities, and death camps—demagogues "of a faith that taught the hatred that was breathed into their faithful ever since the cradle." Acknowledging the few who risked their lives to tear their brothers and sisters away from the fury of the barbarians, he asks:

> Where were the others?
> The millions of others?
> The hundreds of millions of others?
> Their voices died into a great silence,
> the great silence of hatred.
> Gone down into the arena, Rome saw with joy
> the gladiator perish, devoured by the wild beast.
>
> ("The Holocaust")

Christians, according to Taraboulos, learned well the lessons of the Romans and practiced them on the Jews:

> Ah! They have played their hand
> all through the millennia.
> Their sages, muddled by pagan inheritance,
> breathed into them the foul breath
> of a warped conscience,
> declaring human love for the Jew taboo.

He, like other Sephardic poets, is painfully aware of the parallels between the Crusaders, the Spanish Inquisition, and the Holocaust:

Admirable deed that of the ... "Right Holy Inquisition."
Disgrace and damnation.
Crusaders massacring all the Jews in their path,
guided by the fiery word of their monks.

("The Holocaust")

Again, Taraboulos emphasizes that Torquemada and Hitler were not to be surpassed; indeed, they proved worthy of the trust placed in them by the millions of faithful. For carrying out their obligations to perfection, they would be "cursed forever and ever, forever and ever" and damned to "vanish in the hell of oblivion and disgrace" by Sephardic poets and their coreligionists:

Worms, Speyer, Mainz,
and so many other places.
Stars of ill omen, shining with a bloody fire,
have you not guided the steps of the Great Devil?
O Cross of Shame, covered with burned flesh,
have you not borne on your bosom
the Swastika of the Brute?
O Torquemada, of cursed memory,
O Isabella, bitch of misfortune,
O Great Curse, miserable and worthless Nazis,
may your bones be consumed
in fire and shame.

("The Holocaust")

In Elie Wiesel's *Legends of Our Time*, we read that his generation has been robbed of everything, even of their cemeteries. Yehuda Haim Perahia, referring to the destruction of the centuries-old cemetery of Salonika, also bewails the shameful treatment of the dead in "The Second Cry in Anguish":

And the beloved dead, they were also abused.
The world of the Beth Hahaya in which so many rested, illumined
    by God,
Was overturned, sacked, and torn up,
And the beasts with human faces did it all with hideous roaring.

Hitler's move to exterminate the Jews of Europe would have been impossible without the support of his friends and the citizens of the occupied countries. The task was "so enormous, complex, and economically demanding that it took the best efforts of millions of Germans, and later Austrians, Czechoslovakians, Poles, Russians, French, Rumanians, Bulgarians, Slovaks, Hungarians, and Dutch, with the support of the national churches. . . ."[25] Nor, the victims charge, did the Allies and other civilized peoples come to the aid of the Jews.

> The whole world participated in the macabre spectacle
> without trying to save, to help, to punish,
> without being moved by a whole nation dead,
> without giving signs of repentance or even denial.
>
> (Reuven, "Yom Hachoa")

> Where was the world that is considered to be civilized?
> Where were the nations that were fighting for freedom?
> When millions in their blazing torture
> Vanished in smoke, victims of ferocity.
>
> (Reuven, "Salonika")

While the poets of Sepharad denounce the guilty, they praise and immortalize those who, at the cost of their lives and those of their families, came to the aid of the condemned. Such heroes were found throughout the countries of Europe. Among them were members of the Resistance; certain officials of the Catholic, Eastern Orthodox, and Protestant churches; leaders of nations; labor unions; and hundreds of individuals. Their acts of mercy and love in support of the Jew in the midst of local animosity, indifference, and outright anti-Semitism have been commended by the Yad Vashem Institute and by the surviving victims and their coreligionists. By the humane efforts of brave individuals, many children were housed in monasteries, networks for escape were established, and whole families were hidden in the mountains, villages, and cities. Were it not for his Greek Orthodox maid, Anastasia, Yehuda Haim Perahia would have suffered the same tragedy as his Macedonian brothers and sisters, who, it is believed, were drowned in the Danube. Her words of comfort and companionship, while fleeing enemies from city to city, kept him alive:

> Tears run from my eyes and my feet do not stop.
> My faithful Anastasia who has served me for twenty years
> Holds me up to prevent me from falling unconscious
> And letting the evil enemies take me in this mental state.
>
> ("The Third Cry in Anguish in Salonika")

Taraboulos, in spite of his bitterness toward the Christian world and the Western nations, blesses those just individuals from among the hundreds of millions who remained silent. He is aware that we must praise the attitude of these exceptional people, considering the sentiments of abhorrence instilled in them by their society and faith:

> And you, the just among the nations,
> who at the risk of your life,
> forgetting the hatred that your faith had taught you
> and that was breathed into you ever since the cradle,
> have torn my brothers away from the fury of the barbarians.
> Be blessed, be blessed.
> You were a few, a handful of brave men,
> robust and sound seeds,
> full-blown in the soil of love.

("The Holocaust")

The great majority of Europeans were indifferent to or actively supportive of the Holocaust. Most countries took advantage of the situation to improve their economic lot and political position, as well as to satisfy perverse psychological desires at the expense of the perennial scapegoat, the Jew, who had borne the blame for the sins and failures of the Christian world for two thousand years. Bulgaria, an ally of the Third Reich, did save the entire Jewish population of the country in spite of orders to the contrary from Berlin. That nation, however, is guilty of collaboration for participation in the total annihilation of the Macedonian Jewry. Perahia states that on the nights of March 3–4, 1943, the Bulgarians seized all the Jews of Xeres, Drama, Kavalla, Xanthi, Gumulgina, and Dedeagatch. After being robbed of all their possessions, they were taken to Bulgaria, where, according to Perahia and some survivors from Salonika, "They were drowned in the Danube. None of them ever returned."[26]

Denmark occupies a special place for Taraboulos. "The strike by the dock workers and the support of the total population, although temporary, will never be forgotten by the Jewish nation," he told me in an interview in 1982. In "The Holocaust" he wrote,

> And you, O land of Denmark, that was the exception,
> be forever and ever blessed in the bosom of the Eternal.
> Your king, your daughters and your sons,
> your living and your dead,

and the sea that touches your shores,
for having seen so much bravery and love,
may the hand of God be upon you,
and keep you until the end of time.

The sacrifices of those who survived, who have endured humiliation, horror, and indescribable brutality, will not be in vain, for God has always preserved a remnant in the resurrected Israel. Marcel Chalom's book *Jewish Poems* includes "Family Tree" in memory of those who perished in hostile lands. He sees in the surviving child a glorious Israel, rising like a phoenix from the ashes:

My dear Jewish child! Live in glory!
Your mother died in a crematory oven,
　　　Your father lies in Poland
　　　　In a mass grave,
　　　Your brother was still-born . . .
But you, the last bastion,
You are
　　　their
　　　　RESURRECTION!

A statue of a living child feeding at the breast of its dead mother was proposed (but never built) to honor the martyrs from Rhodes and to symbolize God's assurance of the continuity of the faithful, the remaining few, as exemplified years ago in two lines from Chaim

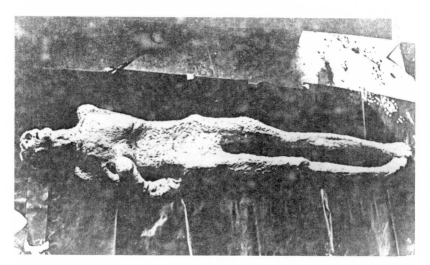

"Death and Hope of Survival." Courtesy of the Jewish community of Rhodes.

Nahman Bialik's "The City of Slaughter": "A story of a suckling child asleep / A dead and cloven breast between its lips."[27] The child holds to the tradition of the past and represents the hope of survival of the Jewish people.

Those who perished in the streets, ghettos, slaughterhouses, and gas chambers gave their lives for the glory of Israel and will always be remembered by their descendants. Henriette Asseo sees the hope of her people on the mountains of bones piled in the death camps. Where Attila was successful in burning forever the grass over which his horsemen rode, Hitler failed. On the corpses of his victims, "only green grass" grows. Chelomo Reuven perceives on the blessed ash and the mountains of bones a great light, a sunbeam that affirms the eternity of the new nation of Israel. This nation lives. It is unshaken and assures God's Chosen that no force will ever destroy it again:

> But over the death camps and from that gray cloud
> grew the delicate flower of our liberation,
> and over the beloved bones and mountains of ash,
> at the cost of new blood, our nation was restored.
>
> Rest, beloved souls, from your last sleep.
> You have fallen. With your death, evil seemed to have conquered,
> but with your breath, you have given life to our genius
> and our lips murmur: "Yitgadal veyitkadash."
>
> ("Yom Hachoa")

The Holocaust is not only the story of the ultimate tragedy that befell the Jewish people but a testimony to the cruelty of humankind, to a horrifying world in which everything went awry, in which religion, morality, and individual and social ethics lost their meaning. Because of excessive preoccupation with themselves and their immediate circle, human beings rejected their own rationality and pragmatism, creating their own fantasies and prejudices which ultimately warped their personal and social behavior. This state of mind, prevalent in Nazi Germany, gave rise to the Holocaust. And unless human frustrations are dealt with on the personal, family, and social levels, and problems resolved, the tragic events of the 1940s in Europe will continue to weigh heavily on all people.

In the words of Marcel Chalom, the Jew prays for a world in which love will reign and neither people nor animals will flee. The Jew—the anathema of the world, symbol of all human suffering, the universal wanderer—yearns for a world in which everyone can "build happiness, peace, civilization with no fear of demolition." Both Jew and Gentile must learn to be more open-minded, more willingly disposed to act effectively against all wrongs, more accessible to the stranger and the homeless. Chalom's "The Prayer of the Persecuted Jew" depicts a universe in which all humanity lives in fellowship and harmony, in which mothers raise their children with no worries, in which people and nature coexist in peace under the guidance of God the Almighty:

> Lord, I want a world
> > Not for me but for my brothers.
> A new world,
> > with no quarrels and no wars,
> With no storms and no thunder
> > to rumble!
>
> Lord, I want a world
> > where the mothers
> Will raise their children
> > with no fear
> Of seeing them suddenly leave . . .
>
> A world where the life that You give
> > will have its value.
> Where spirits will be the same,
> Where men, by way of creed,
> Will only know one utterance:
> > "I love you!"

NOTES

1. Those poets I spoke with told me that the voices in the poems are their own; the feelings expressed by the narrators of the poems are those of the poets themselves.

2. Quoted in Brown, *Elie Wiesel*, p. 201.

3. Wiesel, *Legends of Our Time*, p. 26.

4. Beker, "Don't Show Me."

5. Except for the poem "Vision," by Yehuda Haim Perahia, all excerpts of Sephardic poetry in this chapter are drawn from the translated poems, which appear in their entirety in the section of this book entitled "Sephardic Poetry of the Holocaust." All of Perahia's poems were given to me in manuscript form by Moise Pessah, the poet's nephew.

6. This is one of several works the author gave me in 1982 during my visit to Israel. For the translation of this novel into French, see Chedal, *Le muet d'Auschwitz*. Nancy Kobrin stated in an oral presentation before the

Sephardic section of the Modern Language Association that the novel was translated in 1966 into modern Spanish by Eval Jardiel but was never published.

7. Quoted in Meltzer, *Never to Forget*, p. xvi.

8. See Bauer, *They Chose Life*, p. xvi.

9. Quoted in Syrkin, *Blessed Is the Match*, epigraph.

10. Cohen, *The Tremendum*, p. 2.

11. Fine, *Legacy of Night*, p. xiii.

12. Brenner, *Faith and Doubt*, p. 54. The author provides a detailed study of the attitude of the survivors toward religion.

13. Several scholars have examined the issue of Spain's protection of the Sephardim during World War II. It is clear that the Jews, not exclusively Sephardic, who illegally immigrated from France and Holland found refuge in Spain. However, with respect to the Sephardim who held Spanish passports, acquired in the early 1900s, there was ambivalence. While the Spanish government claimed to be doing all in its power to rescue the descendants of the Jews who had been exiled from Spain four hundred years ago, in reality it did very little. The government placed stipulations on the manner in which Spanish Jews who held valid passports could emigrate; for instance, Jews could not enter en masse, only individually or in small groups, and they had to be self-supporting or have the financial assistance of a benevolent organization. Moreover, even though the Jews were Spanish citizens, they were refused the right to remain in the country. The government insisted that they move on and refused to admit other refugees until the previous ones had left Spain. One must note, however, that the Spanish government did rescue from Bergen-Belsen 367 Jews who held Spanish passports. The majority of these left Spain on June 21, 1944, for Fedhala, a temporary camp near Casablanca. See Avni, "Spanish Nationals in Greece"; Avni, "Rescue Attempts during the Holocaust"; Avni, *Spain, the Jews and Franco*; Gaon, "The Role of Spain."

14. Quoted in Berenbaum, *Vision of the Void*, pp. 111–12.

15. "A kingdom of priests and a holy nation" (Exodus 19).

16. Professor David Altabe informed me of the existence of four poems by an unknown author, later found to be Yehuda Haim Perahia, dealing with the Holocaust. These were attached to the flyleaf of a booklet entitled *Kozas pasadas* belonging to the Sephardic section of Yeshiva University. Altabe's English translations of four of the poems—"The First Cry in Anguish"; "The Second Cry in Anguish"; "The Third Cry in Anguish in Salonika"; "After the Catastrophe in Salonika"—appear in *Sephardic Brother*, no. 1, 19 (Spring 1978), pp. 4–6. The fourth poem was also published in *Le Judasm Sephardi*, April 1959, p. 815, under the title "Endecha, despues de la catastrofa de Salonica."

17. Following is the Judeo-Spanish version, as given to me by Mr. Leon Cohen in Tel Aviv:

> Un viejiziko de muestro puevlo siempre estava asentado en el kampo i rengrasiava al Dio por su mersed i buendad por su puevlo. Todos los dias veia los trenos estefados de djente ayegar. Komo

zahutiero, el rengrasiava al Dio por amenchuguar el grupo. I dezia: "Patron del mundo, tu siempre mantuvites tus prometas de multiplikarmos i ek aki mos estamos multiplikando por dia i por ora, mizmo muestros muertos si van multiplikando. Si, Dio, muestras orasiones tambien si van multiplikando, i tu absensia se esta multiplikando. O Dio, porke no estas tu aki kon mozotros?"

18. Wiesel, "Israel," p. 66.

19. The Judeo-Spanish version:

> Un djoven, kansado de las muchas orores ke el i su puevlo yevavan de dia en dia a las manos de las bestias umanas, demando kual era la parte ke el Dio tenia en los krimenes i su mankansa de traer djustisia a los kampos i de azer sus deveres para su puevlo: "Tio," dizia, "porke todas estas orasiones? Porke meldar el kadish para los muertos, el Dio los protejara mas en el paradizo de lo ke izo en la tyerra?"

> El vyejo se sentava kayado i sentia kon atension. No teniendo dinguna respuestas ke kontentaria ni al djoven ni a si mizmo, estava dakodro ke el Dio era insensitivo i kruel algunas vezis. "Estas demandas deven ser konsideradas," dezia, "ma primero vamos a demandar ke el Dio mos gie."

20. Browne, *How Odd of God*, p. 9.

21. Ibid.

22. Heschel, "The Meaning of This Hour," pp. 491–92.

23. Ibid., p. 491. Berkovits (*Faith after the Holocaust*, p. 106) states that "God [is] waiting for the sinner to find his way to Him." Thus, God is not ready to forgive until His people renounce their way of life and return to Him.

24. For a detailed study on the Christian church's knowledge of the tragedy that the Jews of Europe were suffering at the hands of the Germans and their allies, see Ross, *So It Was True*.

25. Feig, *Hitler's Death Camps*, p. 12. See also Shonfeld, *The Holocaust Victims Accuse*. Rabbi Shonfeld places the blame for the Holocaust on the Western countries, for their indifference; the Eastern countries, for their anti-Semitism; and the Catholic church, for both its participation and its silence.

26. See p. 17, note 15; see also p. 129.

27. *Selected Poems*, p. 233.

Sephardic Poetry of the Holocaust

HENRIETTE ASSEO

A professor at the École Normale Supérieure in Paris, Henriette Asseo, a descendant of Salonikan Jews who emigrated to France, is completing graduate studies in history. Her Jewish education and the knowledge that her father's family and practically all of her mother's perished in the camps stirred in her "a somewhat guilty nostalgia for what had been the life of those who have vanished." Her first work on the subject, "Du miel aux cendres . . . : Ou sont passés 70,000 Juifs de Salonique?" (From honey to ashes . . . : Where have the 70,000 Jews from Salonika gone?) appeared in *Les Temps Modernes* (October-November 1979, pp. 828–45). The poems reproduced here were published in *Vidas Largas* (no. 2, April 1983, pp. 44–46) and appear by permission of Henriette Asseo and the journal's editor, Haim Vidal Sephiha.

Terreur morale

La sombre limite des mots

fait peur

quand le talent n'est pas

qui restitue la mémoire collective

Moral Terror

The somber limitation of words

inspires fear

when talent fails

to restore collective memory.

Attila ecologique

Sur les miens
sur les cadavres des miens
sur les morceaux de cadavres des miens
sur les bribes de cadavres des miens
sur les monceaux de bribes de cadavres des miens
sur les monceaux de morceaux de cadavres des miens
sur les amas de cadavres des miens
à Maïdanek et Auschwitz
à Birkenau et Tréblinka
seule l'herbe
                verte.

Ecological Attila

On my people
on the corpses of my people
on the pieces of the corpses of my people
on the chunks of the corpses of my people
on the piles of the chunks of the corpses of my people
on the piles of the pieces of the corpses of my people
on the heaps of the corpses of my people
in Maidanek and Auschwitz
in Birkenau and Treblinka
only green
                    grass.

Mais qui sait?

L'horreur des camps
il ne faut pas la dire
et puis ça n'intéresse
personne
puisque c'est personne
qui est mort
si c'est pas exprès
pour embêter
c'est le cadavre qui prouve le crime
pas l'officier SS
cela ne fait rien
je saurai bien réciter le Kaddish enfiévré
au-dessus des charniers inaudibles
même si vos âmes occidées
reposent en un sol si meuble
qu'il a eu raison
de vos millions
d'ossements
ils ne célèbrent
que l'herbe de dessus
ceux qui à présent vous nient
croient-ils ainsi trouver le repos?
   les morts non honorés hantent le sommeil des vivants.

But Who Knows?

The horror of the camps
should not be told.
Besides, it is of no concern
to anyone
since no one
died;
it was only done purposely
to annoy.
It is the corpse that proves the crime,
not the SS officer.
It does not matter;
I will be able to recite well the feverish Kaddish
on the silent ossuaries,
even if your slain souls
rest in such a loose soil
that has triumphed over
your millions
of bones.
They sing only the praises
of the grass that sprouted,
those who at present deny you;
do they think they have found peace of mind?
    The dead not honored haunt the sleep of the living.

Mon peuple

Mon peuple vous ne le connaissez pas
jadis l'exodus du luxe
l'a décimé en mille nations

Mon peuple ne vous ressemble pas
servitude de l'alliance
en Dieu identifié

Mon peuple n'existe pas
exil de la mémoire
aux portes des camps

My People

My people you do not know
   in days of old the exodus from ease
   scattered them into a thousand nations.

My people do not resemble you
   followers of the Covenant
   identified with God.

My people do not exist
   banished from memory
   at the gates of the camps.

ITZHAK BEN RUBY

Born in Salonika, Greece, Itzhak Ben Ruby moved to Palestine before
World War II. He was well known to the Sephardim of Israel for his
Judeo-Spanish program on Kol Israel Radio and as the editor of *El
Tiempo*. His vignettes on "Aqui vos avla Chimon, Chimon" (Here
speaks Chimon, Chimon), which represented the new immigrant
after the creation of the state of Israel, reported on many aspects of
life in Israel. He also wrote five novels—one of which, *El sekreto
del mudo* (The secret of the mute), deals with the Holocaust—and
published short stories, poetry, and two plays. His achievements as
a writer and a reporter received recognition in Israel, Europe, and
South America. "Escutcha mi hermano" (Listen, my brother) ap-
peared in *El Tiempo* (April 4, 1962, col. 14, p. 3).

Escutcha mi hermano

Te rogo ke me eskutches,
mi hermano.
Es el uniko favor
ke rekalmo de ti,
en esta notche fria,
komo tu korazon!

Te yamo mi hermano,
Porke los sos;
de raza,
de sangre,
de fey . . .
I algo tengo a desirte
a ti, no a otro;
I kero ke me eskutches,
mi hermano,
imploro tu atension,
en esta notche fria
komo tu korazon!

Dame tu mano i mira,
mira kon mi,
lo ke yo esto viendo:
Ayi, ayi este tchiko
aferrado por los pies
i lanzado kontra la pared . . .
para kaer al suelo
kon su kavesa rota!

Mira, mira.
Por favor, no te espantes . . .
Tu estas trankilo
aki onde bives.
Mira, mira,
ayi, ves estas hijas
desnudas
ke temblan
komo ojas al viento?

Listen, My Brother

I beg you to listen,
my brother.
That is the only favor
I request from you
on this chill night
as cold as your heart.

I call you my brother
because you are;
of lineage,
of blood,
of faith . . .
There is something I must tell you,
you, and no one else.
And I want you to listen,
my brother.
I beseech your attention
on this chill night
as cold as your heart.

Give me your hand and look.
Look with me
at what I am seeing:
there, over there, this child
seized by the feet
and hurled against the wall . . .
to fall to the ground
with a broken head.

Look, look.
Please, do not be afraid . . .
You are at peace,
here where you are.
Look, look,
there, do you see those girls,
naked,
shivering
like leaves in the wind?

Demonios
vomitados del infierno
lanzaron kontra eyas
perros-lovos,
ke apasiguaron sus sed
sexual
sovre sus kuerpos
martirisados!

No te espantes
i mira mas . . .
ayi, ayi, al fondo,
estas flamas
ke suven al sielo
komo un gemido
de la Humanidad entera,
la Humanidad
ferida. . .
kuerpos humanos
de raza,
de sangre,
de fey
ke alimentaron el fuego!

I mira mas ayi
las mitraliosas ke krepitan,
los kuerpos ke kayen,
i los infernales
angeles pretos de la muerte,
arrojar estos kuerpos
en foyas
ke apresuradamente serran
kon paletadas de tierra!

Demons,
spewed out from Hell,
set on them
bloodhounds
who quenched their sexual
thirst
on their martyred bodies

Do not be afraid
and look further . . .
There, over there, in the distance,
those flames
that rise toward the heavens
like a cry
of all humanity—
a wounded
humanity—
human bodies
of your brothers,
of lineage,
of blood,
of faith,
that fed the fire.

And look still further:
the machine guns that riddle,
the bodies that fall,
and the infernal
black angels of death
shove them
into the holes
that they hurriedly cover
with shovelfuls of dirt.

Mira, mira,
Ayi la tierra tembla?
se mueve?
Entre los muertos
enterraron
viktimas ke todavia
bivian ...
a las kualas no dieron
el golpe de grasia,
ke la piedad ordena
mismo para los kriminales!

I ansi murieron
Dos, sinko, sech miliones,
de tus hermanos
de raza,
de sangre,
de fey!

... I agora, vate,
vate i yeva kon ti
tu frio korazon
komo esta notche fria!
Tienes lagrimas a tus ojos?
Ma los yoros no sirvieron!
Vate, vate, mi hermano,
de raza,
de sangre,
de fey!

Te kedas?
Tu mano fria
komo tu korazon
buchka mi mano
i la estretcha?
Tus ojos mas no yoran,
ma me miran i me avlan?

Look, look.
There. The earth shakes?
Does it move?
Among the dead
they buried
victims who were still
alive . . . ,
to whom they did not grant
the mercy stroke
that compassion demands
even for criminals.

And so they died,
two, five, six million
of your brothers
of lineage,
of blood,
of faith.

. . . And now, leave,
leave and take with you
your heart, cold
as this chill night.
Your eyes, are they shedding tears?
Alas. Crying was for nought.
Leave, leave, my brother
of lineage,
of blood,
of faith.

You stay?
Your hand, cold
as your heart,
reaches for my hand
and holds it steadfast?
Your eyes no longer cry,
but look at me and speak?

Kedate!
Vo pasar kon ti
esta notche fria . . .
Ma, maniana,
Oh! maniana!
Un sol resplandesiente
iluminara tus karas,
i mano a mano,
kon pie firme,
kaminaremos, mi hermano,
verdad?
en los kaminos
de la dignidad humana,
i de la Libertad!

Stay.
I shall spend with you
this chill night . . .
But tomorrow,
oh, tomorrow!
A bright sun
will shine on your face,
and hand in hand,
with a firm step,
we shall walk together, my brother,
—shall we?—
on the road
of human dignity
and liberty.

MARCEL CHALOM
(Also known as Soliman Salom)

Born in Edirne, Turkey, Chalom wrote for the *Voz de Oriente* (later the *Voz de Turquía*). After the death of its editor, Albert Cohen, he moved to Paris, where he worked for several years for the Union Sioniste of France as the editor of *L'Echo Sioniste*. He was a professor of Turkish language and literature in the Department of Arabic and Islamic Studies at the Instituto de Estudios Orientales y Africanos, Universidad Autónoma de Madrid. He also contributed to the daily newspaper *Milliyet* of Istanbul. Chalom wrote some twenty critical works on Turkish literature and history and was an avid poet. The poems reproduced here appeared in *Poèmes Juifs* (Istanbul: Becid Basidmevi, 1949).

Arbre généalogique . . .

Mon petit Juif ! Vis dans la gloire !

Ta mère est morte dans un four crématoire,

Ton père est en Pologne,

Dans un fosse commune,

Ton frère fut un mort-né . . .

Mais toi, dernier bastion

tu es

leur

R E S U R R E C T I O N !

Family Tree . . .

My dear Jewish child! Live in glory!

Your mother died in a crematory oven,

Your father lies in Poland

In a mass grave,

Your brother was stillborn . . .

But you, the last bastion,

You are

their

RESURRECTION!

Camp de concentration

Nice—Décembre 1943

Ils étaient trois, le mari, la femme et leur bébé.
Ils étaient trois, avec tant de milliers,
On les a ramassés un beau jour,
On les a mis derrière les barbelés . . .
Ils étaient jeunes et pleins de vie
Pleins de vie comme tous leur frères!
Le père

        s'appelait David. C'est criminel.

Le deuil a pénétré leur coeur comme un appel . . .
Leurs yeux ont brûlé
Au sel intarissable des pleurs.
Ils ont, aux barbelés
Accroché les lambeaux sanglants de leur douleur.
Oh! qu'ils étaient nombreux ces frères d'infortune,
Qui évoquaient les soirs, le fiel du temps passé,
N'ayant pour réchauffer leur coeur, que la lune
Claquant des dents au vent glacé . . .
Ces coeurs se sont éteints comme des fleurs pourries,
Ils ont baigné leurs mains dans une eau sans histoire,
Par leur course forcée vers la mort, ils ont nourri

        Les fours crématoires . . .

Pauvre David tu es parti. C'est là ton sort,
Ton sort comme celui de tant d'autres
Dont le nombre seul donne le vertige . . .
Vous voilà enfouis dans la glace de la mort
En un siècle qui ose

            parler de gloire et de prestige . . .

Oh! mes pauvres, pauvres frères de race,
Vous n'avez point mérité
Qu'on vous abatte, comme des chiens, sans vous compter . . .
Par la faute de ce recul inconsolable de l'humanité.

Concentration Camp

Nice—December 1943

They were three of them: the husband, the wife, and their baby.
They were three, with so many thousands,
They picked them up one fine day,
They put them behind the barbed wire . . .
They were young and full of life,
Full of life like all their brethren.
The father's

     name was David. It is criminal.

Sorrow penetrated their hearts like a cry.
Their eyes burned
With the never-ending salt of the tears.
On the barbed wire
They hung the bloody shreds of their pain.
Oh! They were many, these brothers of misfortune,
Who remembered at night the bitter gall of past times,
Having only the moon to warm their hearts,
Their teeth chattering in the icy wind . . .
Their hearts wilted like rotten flowers.
They washed their hands in a water without history.
By their forced marches to death, they fed

     The furnaces of the crematoria . . .

Poor David, you are gone. That is your fate,
Your fate like that of so many others
Whose very numbers drive one mad . . .
There you are buried in the ice of death
In a century that dares

     Speak of glory and prestige . . .

Oh, my poor, poor Jewish brethren,
You did not deserve
To be struck down like dogs, unreckoned . . .
Because of this wretched retreat of humanity.

La prière du Juif persécuté

Seigneur, je veux un monde
    Non pas pour moi, pour mes frères,
Un monde nouveau,
    sans querelles et sans guerres,
Sans orages et sans tonnerres
    Qui grondent!

Seigneur, je veux un monde,
    où les mères
Elèveront leurs enfants,
    sans la crainte
De les voir partir soudainement . . .

Un monde où la vie que vous donnez
    aura son prix.
Où les esprits seront les mêmes,
Où les hommes en guise de symbole,
Ne connaîtront qu'une parole:
    "Je vous aime!"

Seigneur, je veux un monde,
Sans étés, sans hivers,
Sans montagnes et sans abîmes,
Je veux que dans mon univers,
Tous ceux qui peinent et tous ceux qui triment
Aient le droit de vivre
Sans qu'on les oblige à se battre
    Pour avoir la force de mourir! . . .

Dans ce monde, si vous me le donnez,
Je veux que le printemps
    Comble tous les instants
      De l'année . . .

The Prayer of the Persecuted Jew

(Translated by Rosemary Lévy Zumwalt)

Lord, I want a world
    Not for me but for my brothers.
A new world,
    with no quarrels and no wars,
With no storms and no thunder
        to rumble!

Lord, I want a world
        where the mothers
Will raise their children
    with no fear
Of seeing them suddenly leave . . .

A world where the life that You give
        will have its value.
Where spirits will be the same,
Where men, by way of creed,
Will only know one utterance:
        "I love you!"

Lord, I want a world
With no summers, with no winters,
With no mountains and no chasms.
I want in my universe
All who suffer and all who toil
To have the right to live
Without being forced to fight
    For the strength to die! . . .

In this world, if You give it to me,
I want spring
    To fill all the moments
        Of the year . . .

Dans ce monde énigmatique,
Les oiseaux aux chants mélancoliques
Ne fuiront plus les êtres humains!
On construira partout,
    Le bonheur, la paix, la civilisation,
    Sans crainte de la démolition!...

Chacun suivra alors, sans haine et sans envie
La route
    qu'il voudra se tracer dans la vie ...
Toutes
    les professions seront respectées,
Le travailleur et le poète,
Le rentier et l'architecte,
Chacun posera un pavé

    sur la route immense
        de la tranquilité rêvée ...

Le pas de danse,
    remplacera le pas de guerre.
Dans les bouches des canons,
    rouillés par l'abandon,
        les oiseaux auront construit
        leurs petits nids ...

Nous n'aurons plus d'inventeurs
    d'engins et de moteurs
        à prendre l'âme! ...
Vous seul Seigneur, nous la prendrez,
        quand vous voudrez! ...

In this enigmatic world,
Birds with melancholy songs
Will no longer flee from human beings.
Everywhere will be built
 Happiness, peace, civilization,
 With no fear of demolition! . . .

Each one will then follow, with no hate and no envy,
The road
 that he wants to pursue in life . . .
All
 professions will be respected,
The laborer and the poet,
The stockholder and the architect,
Each one will lay a pavingstone

 on the measureless road
  of the tranquility of dreams . . .

The dance step
 will replace the march step of war.
In the mouths of cannons,
 rusted in disuse,
 the birds will have built
  their little nests . . .

We will have no more inventors
 of engines and motors
  to take life! . . .
Only You, Lord, will take it from us
  whenever You wish! . . .

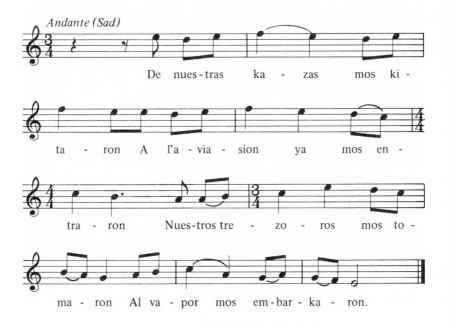

Musical rendition of "La vida de los Djudios en 1944."

VIOLETTE MAYO FINTZ

A survivor from the German extermination camps, Violette Mayo Fintz was born on the island of Rhodes and presently lives in Sea Point (Cape Town), South Africa. In spite of her busy schedule, she unselfishly gives her time and effort to the many scholars and lay-people who constantly inquire about the tragedy that befell the Jews of the Dodecanese Islands. Her experiences have been published in several newspapers; the last interview by Gorry Bowes-Taylor appeared in *The Argus* of Cape Town on March 7, 1985. She has participated in several celebrations of Yom Hashoa (Day of Remembrance) and in various conferences to keep alive the memory of the obliterated Jewish centers. "I cry over the fate of all Jews," she told me. "I cannot forget the agony, I refuse to forget the sting of death in the camps. I shall always remember the faces of the thousands of innocent children, of our children. I want the world to know that the Sephardim were also martyrs and that we, too, saw our towns destroyed and our families vanish in the smoke." During our meeting in Brussels and through a long correspondence, she has provided me with several testimonies and poems written by other survivors from Rhodes, including the anonymous poem "Qui in questa terra" (Here in this land), composed by a group of young women from Rhodes. Sara Mayo Menasche, now living in Brussels, assisted with the composition of the poem "La vida de los Djudios en 1944" (The life of the Jews in 1944).

La vida de los Djudios en 1944

De muestras kazas mos kitaron,
A l'aviasion ya mos entraron,
Nuestros trezoros mos tomaron,
Al vapor mos enbarkaron.

Al vapor ya entrimos,
Komo sardelas mos estefimos,
Diez dias navegimos,
A Pireos dezbarkomos.

A Pireos dezbarkomos,
komo los peros arastimos,
Munchos keridos aya pedrimos,
Para Haydar prosegimos.

A Haydar ya arevimos,
De haftonas mos konsomimos,
Tres dias estovimos,
De ansias mos abatimos.

Al tren ya mos entraron,
Sin komer mos desharon,
Katorze dias viajimos,
A Auschwitz dezbarkimos.

In Auschwitz mos dezbarkaron,
Kon nuestros keridos mos separaron,
Al banyo mos entraron,
Los kaveyos mos kortaron.

Los kaveyos mos kortaron,
Dezmudas mos desharon,
Los vestidos mos tomaron,
Al bloko vente mos mandaron.

A las tres de media noche,
Al bloko vente ya arevimos,
Los apelos empesaron,
I los frios mos aporaron.

The Life of the Jews in 1944[1]

From our homes they removed us,
In the Airport[2] they put us,
Our treasures they took from us,
Onto the boats they loaded us.

Onto the boats we boarded,
Like sardines we pressed together,
Ten days we were sailing,
In Piraeus we disembarked.

In Piraeus we disembarked,
Like dogs we dragged ourselves,
Many loved ones we lost there,
And to Haydar we proceeded.

To Haydar we then came,
From beatings we were worn out,
Three days we spent there,
With anguish we were afflicted.

Onto the trains they put us,
Without food they left us,
For fourteen days we traveled,
In Auschwitz we descended.

At Auschwitz they put us out,
From our loved ones they separated us,
Into the baths they put us,
Our hair they cut off.

Our hair they cut off,
Naked they left us,
Our clothes they took away,
To Block Twenty they sent us.

At three o'clock in the morning,
At Block Twenty we arrived,
The roll calls began,
And the cold wore us out.

A Auschwitz kon haftunas,
Al apelo mas i mas,
Bloko Vashtuva kon kalamedad,
Mos arivaron sin piadad.

Yorando noche i dia,
Yamando siempre: "Madre mia!"
Mos fue dicho i asigurado,
Ke en el fuego fueron kemados.

En el gas asfiksiando
O en el fuego fueron kemados;
Las kreaturas sen pekado,
Al son de la muzika fueron kemados.

Dizgrasiado a Auschwitz,
Ke rovino muestras famiyas,
Ambizados a mucho i bueno,
Arastados sen manzia.

Los trasportos mos kavzaron,
En lage i lage mos rodiaron,
A la fin de la trachedia,
Belsemor mos yevaron.

Belsen tomba umana,
Onde pedrimos muestras ermanas,
Se depedrieron munchas muchachas,
Por la ambre, la mala vida.

No ay tinta ne papel,
Para deskrivir la vida de Belsen;
Kashkara de rapo,
I agua en muerte a bever.

At Auschwitz battered we arrived,
The roll calls kept increasing,
For our misfortune to Waschstube Block,
They brought us pitilessly.

Weeping night and day,
Shouting constantly, "Mother dear!"
We were told and assured,
That they were consumed in the fire.

In the gas chambers asphyxiated,
Or burned in the fire,
Children without sin,
To the sound of music were burned.

Disastrous Auschwitz,
That ruined our families,
Who were used to the best in life,
Dragged off without compassion.

They put together trains for us,
From camp to camp they moved us,
At the end of the journey,
They took us to that Belsen bog.

Belsen, human grave,
Where we lost our sisters,
Great numbers of young women died,
From hunger and a wretched life.

There is neither ink nor paper,
To describe the life in Belsen,
Turnip peelings,
And at death water to drink.

"Sarcophagus"/"The Train," by Evangelos I. Moustakas of Pallini, Greece.
Courtesy of the sculptor.

HIZKIA M. FRANCO

One of the leaders of the Jewish community of Rhodes who received
the title Comendatore della Corona d'Italia, Hizkia M. Franco served
as community president before the deportation to Poland. During
the Nazi occupation of the island he took refuge in Turkey and then
in Israel, returning in 1946 to dedicate himself to literature. He
collaborated with the *Voz de Turquía* and was one of the editors of
the Turkish weekly *Sélam*. He wrote poetry and several prose works,
among them *Empressiones y reflexiones* (Impressions and thoughts)
in Judeo-Spanish. In honor of his devastated city and dead brothers
and sisters, Franco published *Les martyrs Juifs de Rhodes et de Cos*
(Elisabethville: Imbelco, 1952). The poem "La deportacion" (The
deportation) appears on pages 117 and 118 of that work.

La déportacion

Es penible, lastimosa,
Esta triste deportacion,
Tragedia horrorosa
Que me llena de emocion.

Cuanto pueblo, gentirio
Arrancados de sus nogar.
De pensar me toma frio
Al saverlos en el lagar.

Padres, madres, criaturas
Trespisaron sin piadad.
Duras fueron la torturas
Por todo sexo y edad.

Ahogaron tiernos ninios
Sin desturvo ni corazon.
Del cevo de estos lirios
Hicieron guay ! sus buen jabon!

—Que pensas tu O ! San Pablo !
   d'este crimen monstruoso ?
—Pensamiento del Diablo
   lugubre y mansilloso.

No tienen madres ni hijos
estos espiritus del mal ?
No tiene pues ni bitijos
O ! este genio infernal ?

En los hornos crematorios
Masacro grande de judios.
Que murieron en martirios
En tu nombre, O ! Santo Dios !

O ! Auschwitz ! triste, escura !
Sos mancha inembarrable.
Que empania tu figura.
Sos monstre, imperdonable !

The Deportation

It is painful, pitiful,
This sad deportation,
Horrifying tragedy
That fills me with emotion.

How many people, masses,
Uprooted from their homes.
Thinking of it chills me
To know they are in the camps.

Fathers, mothers, children,
They crushed with no pity.
Hard were the tortures
For all sexes and ages.

They smothered tender children
With no emotion or heart.
From the wax of these lilies
They produced, alas! their good soap.

—What do you think, O Saint Paul,
   of this monstrous crime?
—Whim of the Devil,
   somber and pitiable.

Have they no mothers or children
These spirits of evil?
Have they even no stepchildren,
Oh! this infernal spirit?

In the ovens of the crematoria:
Great massacre of Jews
Who died martyrs
In Your Name, O Holy God!

O Auschwitz! sad and gloomy,
You are an ineradicable blemish
That blots out your face.
You are a monster, unforgettable!

Es un crimen sin ejemplo
En la humana historia.
En tu cueva, lindo templo,
Cantaran tu triste gloria.

Que vean bien cual fue en fin
Esta grande desventura
Que miren pues cual fue la fin
De esta mal aventura.

It is a crime without equal
In human history.
In your vault, wonderful temple,
Will be sung your sad glory.

May it be plain what was the end
Of this great misfortune:
That they may see what was the end
Of this evil venture.

DAVID HAIM

David Haim, originally from Salonika, now resides in Tel Aviv, Israel. While I was interviewing him on his experiences in the camps and after the liberation, he gave me a handwritten copy of the poem "Siete dias enserados" (Seven days locked up), which he wrote and read on Kol Israel Radio in 1981, on the anniversary on the Day of Remembrance. Haim has also written poems on other themes in Judeo-Spanish, Greek, and Hebrew.

Siete dias enserados

Siete dias enserados
en vagones de bemas
ouna ves alos tres dias
mos quitavan ayrear.

Madre mia my querida
ya touvites el zehout
de mouerirte en tous tieras
y non passates por el olouk.

Padre mio my cerido
quien te lo iva dezir
que vinieras con tou ermano
al cramatorio de Auchvits.

Padre y madre ermanos y ermanikas
saliendo todos redjadjis
a el patron de el moundo
que embie saloud amy
que me quite de estos campos
para vos etchar kadich!

Seven Days Locked Up

Seven days locked up
in boxcars for animals;
once every three days
they would take us out for air.

My dearest mother,
you were fortunate
in dying in your country
and not passing through the chimney.

My dearest father,
who would have told you
that you would come with your brother
to the crematorium of Auschwitz!

Father and mother, brothers and sisters,
may you all be supplicants
to the Master of the world
to grant me health
and remove me from these camps
to recite for you the Kaddish!

EVELYNE KADOUCHE

Born in Casablanca, Morocco, Evelyne Kadouche was twenty when the Editions Debresse of Paris published a collection of her poems, *Sineuses*. At twenty-four she was the producer of a program on women and a reporter for the Radiodiffusion Télévision Marocaine. A member of the Théatre Marocain, she represented that body before several international conferences and colloquia. In 1971 she moved to Paris, where she held several readings, including one in 1980 at the Centre Georges Pompidou during the Journées de Cultures Juives Orientales Méditerranéennes. In 1984 she represented France before UNESCO at the Journée Internationale de la Femme. Her latest work, in memory of her grandmother, Rachel Cohen, is a collection of poems, *Féminité Sud*. Because of her closeness to her grandmother and her strong Jewish background, Evelyne Kadouche feels the repression and rejection of her people. The poem "Mon sang" (My blood), published in 1985 in the *Tribune Juive*, is her memorial to those who suffered and died at the hands of the Germans.

Mon sang[3]

mon sang gradins

    tournesol de soufre

        initié de lui-même

et d'étoiles jaunies

évanoui – glacé – électrisé

            et rejailli

mon sang qui ne cesse d'avouer

          réfugié et enfui

désarçonné   casqué

poreux et animalier

        disséminé

          fléché

comme un cancrelat pétri

saupoudré de cumin de curry

mon sang moisi
serti de milices vert-de-gris

hululements de sulfure   mon sang cyanure
mon sang dans vos cadastres

          et dans vos quadratures

tatoué de ghettos   mon sang étau
où s'impriment les prisons

        les quartiers généraux

My Blood

(Translated by Marion Attali
and Flora Velluet)

my blood bleachers

    sulphur sunflower

        self-initiated

with yellowed stars

fainting – chilled – electrified

            and gushing

my blood ever confessing

        in refuge and in flight

fleeing down   armor-clad

porous and animalistic

        scattered

          splattered

like a beetle crushed flat

sprinkled with cumin and curry

my blood moldy
verdigris militia set

howling sulphide   my blood cyanide
my blood in your cadastres

        and in your quadratures

tatooed by ghettos   my blood crushed
imprinted by prisons

        stamped by headquarters

mon sang caméléon
                    et de saisons des pluies
mon sang mousson   mon sang cherguy
expulsé   exporté   et enfoui

mon sang en crue en rivières infinies

mon sang peuplade brunâtre et cramoisi

mon sang cohorte   et mon sang colonie
analphabète assassiné mon sang défi
                              Il vit

        . . . mais ses cris déteignent

                        Mars 1980
                        (Féminité Sud)

my blood chameleon
                    from rainy seasons
my blood monsoon   my blood cherguy
expelled   exported   concealed

my blood swelling in endless rivers

my tribal blood crimson-brown

my blood cohort   my blood colony
analphabet assassinated my blood defies
                                It lives

                        . . . but smears with its cries

                        March 1980
                        (Femininity South)

ESTHER MORGUEZ ALGRANTE

A prolific author and the direct descendant of Talmudic scholars, Esther Morguez Algrante has a love for Judaism and the Jewish people, as well as for life in her native Smyrna (Turkey), that is evident in her works. Although she had only a high school education, she studied the Torah and other religious writings under the tutelage of her parents. At the age of twelve she was giving lectures, mainly written by Yaakov Algrante, before the full membership of the Portuguese Synagogue of her native city. Her days were spent working on behalf of the youth of the city. She was the founder of the Committee of the Ladies of the Old Age Home and dedicated thirty-five years of her life to that organization. More than one thousand poems, as well as her articles, were in demand by several popular Judeo-Spanish newspapers, such as *La Vera Luz* of Istanbul, *El Tiempo* of Israel, and the weekly *Şalom* of Istanbul. Many of her works also appeared in Egyptian and European newspapers. Her book of poetry, *9 Eylül: Poesias* (Istanbul: Baski Baykar, 1975), from which the poems reproduced here are taken, questions the tragedy that befell her people in general and specifically the death of six million fellow Jews.

Mis refleksiones sovre el Geto de Varsovia

En kada agno en la mezma data
Mis pensadas non me deşan repozo,
Eyas, se prezentan siempre i sin falta,
Delantre de mis ojos en un tablo afrozo.

Imajes terifiantes vienen sobito,
Trublar mi esfuegno kon tenasidad,
De la agoniya terivle ke el nazi preparo
A mis ermanos matados kon tanta krueldad.

I a la ora, mi epröv empesa ansi :
Mi konsensya me interoja kon insistensya ?
Ayde. Avla. Responde. Porke kedates aki ?
Kuando seş miliones perdieron sus egzistensya ?

Il remorso "EL" me dikta kon fortaleza,
Toma el dolio, aze penitensya, yora,
Implora por esta desdiça, por esta başeza
Por esta matansa unika en la historya.

Seş miliones de ojos sovre mi son fiksados,
Yo non topo a eyos kualo responder ?
Seş miliones de inosentes kemados
Angustia desgrasiada, imposible a venser.

O. Dio. Komo permetites esta kalamitad ?
Komo dates esta fuersa a un maldiço ?
O. Dio. Kastiga te rogo kon krueldad
Ken a tu puevlo eskojido esto izo.

Viejos. Mansevos i tiernas kreaturas,
Siempre estaş gravadas en nuestra alma.
Neşamot adoloriadas en la altura,
Soş apresyadas, alavadas kon fama.

Por non aver nunka perdido vuestra fey.
Vuestra kreyensa en un uniko Dio.
Por aver respektado kon dignitad su Ley.
I luçado fin ke vuestro reflo se perdio.

My Thoughts on the Warsaw Ghetto

Each year on that same day
My thoughts grant me no rest.
Unfailingly they present themselves
Before my eyes in a ghastly tableau.

Horrifying figures come suddenly
Stubbornly to disturb my sleep
Of that terrifying Nazi-contrived agony
For my brothers killed with such brutality.

Immediately my trial begins thus,
My conscience questions me incessantly:
"Well, now, speak, answer. Why are you still alive,
When six million lost their lives?"

God sternly charges me to feel remorse:
"Go into mourning, do penance, lament,
Grieve for this disaster, for this wickedness,
For this slaughter unique in history."

Six million eyes are fixed on me
And I find no answer.
Six million innocent burned!
—Wretched grief, impossible to suppress.

O God! How could You permit such a catastrophe?
How could You grant power to a monster?
O God! I implore You to punish cruelly
The one who did this to Your Chosen.

You, the aged, the adolescents, the tender infants
Are always engraved in our hearts.
Suffering souls now in Heaven,
Forever cherished, in memory praised.

For never having lost your faith,
Your belief in the One God,
For having honored with dignity His Law
And fought until your breath was stilled.

Sielos. Anjelos. Exklamad por eyos vos rogo.
Los martirios inubliables de este puevlo cudyo.
Resitad el kadiş a boz alta i kon yoro
Por estas almas donde la muerte nos enluto.

Ansi . . . En kada agno de eyos me akodrare
De mis ermanos torturados i kemados.
Kon eskritas i elejiyas a eyos yorare
Porke en mi korason siempre son gravados.

BARUH DAYAN AEMET

Heavens. Angels. Cry out for them, I pray,
The never-to-be-forgotten martyrs of the Jewish nation.
Recite the Kaddish aloud and weep
For these souls whom Death brought us to mourn.

Thus . . . Every single year I will remember
My tortured and burned brothers.
With writings and elegies I will lament them,
For in my heart they remain forever engraved.

BLESSED BE THE TRUE JUDGE

En la memoria del Geto de Varsovia

Ya se izo denoçe, todo esta bien eskuro,
Mis pensadas non me deşan repozar,
Imajes teribles sürjisen en mi trublo,
I a la ora komo mis avuelos desido de me levantar.

A media noçe me levanto kon grande anxia
Por yorar i resitar komo lo izo Yirmiya
El profeta ke deplorava nuestra desgrasia
En versos ke revetiyan forma de tefila.

Mi alma bolta verso las tombas de los desparesidos.
I de ayi siento las bozes ke me demandan.
Porke nozotros fuimos maltratados, depedridos ?
Porke ke seyamos kemados ? Kon angustia me reklaman.

Todos eyos repozan en la montagna de Ponar.
En los foyos de Dauttmergen, Belsen i la Estoniya.
I munços i munços otros kampos onde fueron a agonizar.
En Dachau, Stutthof, Kuremes, sentros de esta trajediya.

Eroes kayidos en el Ghetto de Varsoviya.
Mansevos, muçaças onor de nuestra rasa.
Guiborim indomptables yenos de enerjiya,
Vozotros kombatiteş komo soldados de alta klasa.

ANJELOS DE LOS SIELOS POR ESTOS MARTIRIOS
    AZED ORASION.
PORKE SUS ALMAS REPOZEN EN OLAM ABA
VIKTIMAS INOSENTES SIEMPRE GRAVADAS EN
    NUESTRO KORASON
POR VOZOTROS DIZIMOS YITGADAL VE YITKADAŞ
    ŞEME RABA.

In Memory of the Warsaw Ghetto

Night has fallen, everything is quite dark,
My thoughts do not let me rest,
Terrible images spring up in my trouble.
Forthwith, like my ancestors, I decide to get up.

At midnight I get up with great anxiety
To cry and pray like Jeremiah
The prophet deploring our misfortune
In verses dressed in the form of a prayer.

My soul turns toward the graves of the dead,
Whence I hear the voices asking me:
"Why were we mistreated, destroyed?"
"Why were we burned?" they cry out to me in distress.

They all rest in the mountain of Ponar,[4]
In the graves of Dautmergen, Belsen, and Estonia,
And many other camps where they went to die,
In Dachau, Stutthof, Kuremes, centers of this tragedy.

Fallen heroes in the Ghetto of Warsaw,
Young men and women, the pride of our race,
Unconquerable champions full of energy,
You fought like noble warriors.

HEAVENLY ANGELS, FOREVER PRAY FOR THESE
    MARTYRS,
FOR THEIR SOULS TO REST AMONG THE JUST.
INNOCENT VICTIMS ETERNALLY ETCHED IN
    OUR HEARTS,
FOR YOU WE RECITE "YITGADAL VEYITKADASH
    SHEMEI RABA."[5]

A las viktimas del Ghetto de Varsovi

Los sielos de nuves pretas se kuvieron.
La Natura en dolio yora sin kedar.
Miles de mansevos en el fuego murieron.
Dio Grande dime ? Porke a eyos kijites exterminar ?

Jovinas ermozas en siniza trokadas.
Ijas de valor del mundo desparesidas.
Flores freskas muy presto arankadas.
Dio grande dime ? Porke sovre eyas estas firidas ?

Çikos minios a la sonriza dulse i ermoza.
Anjelikos sin pekados de los balkones roncados.
Porke ke vuestra suerte seya tan dolorioza.
Dio grande dime ? Porke eyos fueron matados ?

Talmide Hahamim ke por nozotros rogavan.
A los ornos ardientes fueron eçados.
Ombres ke la Providensya siempre adoravan.
Dio grande dime ? Porke ke eyos tambien seyan kamados ?

Viejos i viejas, por vozotros non uvo piyadad.
Füziyados, matados, kemados, tala fue vuestra triste suerte.
Enemigo salvaje ke non respekto mezmo la edad.
Dio grande dime ? Porke a eyos esta kruel muerte ?

Anjelos de los sielos, por estos heroes siempre azed orasion.
Porke sus almas repozen en Olam Aba.
Viktimas inosemtes siempre gravadas en nuestro korason.
Por vozotros dizimos : Yitgadal ve Yitkadaş şeme raba.

To the Victims of the Warsaw Ghetto

The skies were covered with dark clouds.
Nature in mourning cried unceasingly.
Thousands of youths perished in the fire.
O, Great God! Tell me: Why did You want to exterminate them?

Lovely maidens reduced to ashes.
Precious daughters vanished from Earth.
Blooming flowers untimely cut.
O, Great God! Tell me: Why upon them these wounds?

Infants with pleasant and graceful smiles.
Innocent angels hurled from balconies.
Why should your fate be so agonizing?
O, Great God! Tell me: Why were they killed?

Learned rabbis who prayed for us.
Cast were they into the fiery furnace.
Men who eternally revered their God.
O, Great God! Tell me: Why were they, too, annihilated by fire?

To you old men and old women no mercy was shown.
Shot at, slain, burned, such was your sad fate.
Savage enemy who respected not even age.
O, Great God! Tell me: Why their brutal death?

Heavenly Angels, forever pray for these heroes.
For their souls to rest among the Just.
Innocent victims eternally etched in our hearts.
For you we recite: "Yitgadal veyitkadash shemei raba."

YEHUDA HAIM AARON
HaCOHEN PERAHIA

The representative of a tobacco company with headquarters in Xan-thi, Yehuda Haim Perahia, with the assistance of his maid, spent the war years in hiding in Athens. His devotion to Judaism, his religious background, and his fervor for the political future of the Jews were the main inspiration for his prose and poetry. Among his writings are the novels *Bimba* and *El ultimo esforso,* the monograph *La famille Perahia a Thessaloniki,* a book of poetry entitled *Poemas,* as well as lectures and commentaries on his family and on Judaism in and around Salonika. (Perahia continually copied all his works by hand, often making orthographic changes and commenting on previous statements.) His genealogy dates back to Josephus and the early arrival of the Jews in Spain. The Spanish Inquisition forced a move to Italy, where his family became famous in the rabbinate and in the sciences, especially after they came under the protection of the Sultan in Salonika. After his death, Perahia left his nephew Moise Pessah of Kavalla in charge of his library, and it was Pessah who turned over several manuscripts to me.

Tristeza

Dé mis ojos ounflados dé yorar caillen lagrimas caillentès
Mi alma en péna esta tristé i soufré dé dolorès ardientès
O DIO ! da al moundo ké yora la ménestériza consolation
Los destinos dé los ombrès estan siempré en tou disposition !

Mé bolto à dérécia non topo dingoun rémédio à mi dolor
Mé bolto à destiédra inè para mi ès todo la mezma color
O DIO ! di basta à mouestro apréto i à mouestra désolation
Ten piadad dé tous siervos miramos con ojos dé compassion !

La angoustia i la tristéza non médéchan nada espérar
El souflo sé afoga en mi garganta non mé décha respirar
O DIO ! empénétravlès son tous sécrétos i tous rijos
Ayouda à conosser la ventoura à mi i à todos tous ijos !

Xanthie 15 Chevat 5701
12 Février 1941—Mercredi

Sadness

From my eyes swollen with crying fall warm tears.
   My tormented soul is sad and suffers from burning pain.
   O God! Give to the weeping world the needed consolation.
   The destiny of men is always at Your disposal!

I turn to my right and I find no remedy to my pain.
   I turn to my left, still for me it all looks the same.
   O God! Put an end to our suffering and to our desolation.
   Have pity on Your servants and look upon us with eyes of
      compassion!

Anguish and sadness leave me nothing to hope for.
   The breath stops in my throat and does not let me breathe.
   O God! Mysterious are Your secrets and Your deeds.
   Help me and all Your children to know our future.

Xanthi, 15 Shevat 5701
12 February 1941—Wednesday

Ouna respouesta

Amigo, mé démandas porké mos présighen à mouerté
Somos nos tanto pékadorès por meresser esta souerté ?
Por coualo el DIO mos tomo por ser sou Pouevlo escojido
I somportar por esto tourtouras i sourfiensas sin limito ?

Lo ké démandas en pocos biervos rézolvido non puedé ser
Ay tantas i tantas répouestas bazadas i convensientes à azer
I yo non tengo por aclararlas entéra i yéna la compétenssia
En el rijo del moundo véo en todo la mano dé la Providenssia

A esta Fouersa Potenté i invizivlé esta todo sotomitido ;
El ghio dé la Natoura como dé los ombrès bivos el deztino.
Nada i dingoun mouvimiento pouédé fouillir à sou attention
Sou ojo pénétra en todo, sigouendo del Moundo la Rotation.

Nouestros savios à meldar dia i notché mos encomendaron
A embézar las Sensias dé todo modo i djéniro mos poucharon
Non mitiéron limito à estos embézamientos sin rouydo
Afin dé pouéder pénétrarmos al fondo dé lo dézconossido.

Dezconosido para nouestro intelecto, ma non para el DIO
En la immensita del moundo el solo poudé dizir: So YO
Mozotros non contamos por nada en esta Louz Immensa
Ké intché el Ouniverso i ké forma esta Grandé Fouersa.

A El solamenté appartiénen todas las Encouviertas.
El non da conto à dingouno. Ma, dé por las dezcouviertas
Mos mostro el camino yévando à la vertoud complida
Déchandomos libéros dé sigouirlo o tomar la caréra piédrida.

Como Djidios ténémos tantos dovérès à intchir i à aplikar.
Es ké non mos alondjimos dé eillos en lougar dé mos aserkar ?
Estamos todos limpios dé pékados en mouestra conssenssia ?
Es ké non ténémos nada à réprocharmos verso la Providenssia ?

A Reply

Friend, you ask me why they hounded us to death,
Are we such sinners to merit this fate?
Why did God take us to be His chosen people
And for that reason bear endless tortures and sufferings?

What you ask cannot be resolved in a few words;
Many, there are so very many, basic and convincing answers to
     give.
I do not possess complete and absolute competence to clarify
     them.
In all the workings of the universe I see the hand of Providence.

To this mighty and invisible power everything is subjected;
The mover of the world and of living men's destinies.
Not a single thing or movement can escape His attention;
His eye penetrates everything, following the world's rotation.

Our sages advised us to read day and night;
To master all sciences, they urged us.
Unquestionably, they set no limits to these studies,
In order for us to penetrate the depths of the unknown.

Unknown to our intellect, but not to God,
In the vastness of the world only He can say: "I am."
We are of no value whatsoever in this Immense Light
That fills the Universe and forms this Great Force.

To Him alone belong all secrets.
He answers to none. But through signs
He showed us the way to perfect virtue,
Leaving us free to follow Him or take the road to perdition.

As Jews we have many duties to perform and fullfil.
Is it not that we strayed from them instead of approaching them?
Is our conscience cleared of our sins?
Is it that we have nothing to reproach ourselves for before
     Providence?

Lo ké non maldicho el DIO non pouédé ser malditcho
Proclamo el grandé pagano el famozo Bilam el malditcho.
Lo ké non ménospressio El DIO non pouédé ser ménospréssiado.
Ma mozotros, Caro amigo, non lavorimos por azer nouestro
  Estado.
Ké el Criador méta sou Mano i sé apiadé dé todos mozotros
I ké Israël véa presto sou salvation i akeilla de los otros.

Cavalla, 29 Tamuz 5702
14 Juillet 1942

Al amigo Haim Chémouel Tchimino

What God has not cursed cannot be cursed,
Proclaimed the great pagan, the renowned Bilam, the accursed.
What God has not scorned cannot be scorned.
But we, dear friend, did not labor to attain our condition.
May the Creator raise His hand and have mercy on us all;
And may Israel soon witness her salvation in that of other
    nations.

Kavalla, 29 Tamuz 5702
14 July 1942—Tuesday

To my friend Haim Chemouel Tchimino

Ouna dezgrassia

Sétenssia crouéla dada por arancarlo dé la vida
I presto presto al emprovisto la coza foué éxécoutida
Samaël, el crouel angel dé la mouerté coria i triomfava
Ma Matatron yorava, empontenté dé non pouder azer nada .

Yorar yorava akeilla notché esta madré dezconsoladda
Atabafava sous gimidos adientro sous alma adoloriada
Dizidmé vozotros, si ay mas grandé dolor ké esta dolor
Akéilla dé ouna madré dézijada por el Dio en folor .

Mezmo los mas crouélès non poudian déténersen de yorar
Sous corassonès dezbrociavan en djimidos i exclamar
Deztrouillo el Dio i non sé apiado dé esté soufrenté
Lo acapararon la escouridad i la solombra dé mouerté .

Non poudiamos créeér lo ké nouestros oillidos sentian
Pacharos non giungiuléavan los gaillos todos dourmian
El son luguvré dé la mouerté del innocenté souvia al Ciélo
Mi ojo, mi ojo coré agoua i non pouédé tener esfouénio .

Tou Adonay, sétensiatès esto, dizia el bouen Matatron
Eliaou Anavy couriendo démandava si pouedia aver salvation
Los Angélès i à sous cavésséras Rafaël i Mihaël non avlavan
Ma todos psalmodiavan, vertian lagrimas i endeciavan .

Viéron los angoustiadorès tanta dezgrassia i manzia
Akeilla notché la tomé tiniévla ni séa agiuntada à dia
Escouréssio el DIO nouestras almas i mouestras vistas
Entéros mos acaparo el limounio como salidos dé izbas .

A Tragedy

A cruel judgment was handed down to uproot him from life,
    And promptly, without warning, the sentence was carried out.
    Samael, the cruel Angel of Death, ran in triumph,
    But Matatron cried, powerless, impotent to help.

Tears she kept shedding that night, this disconsolate mother.
    She kept suppressing her moans within her grieving soul.
    Tell me if there is a greater pain than that
    Of a mother separated from her offspring by God in a rage.

Even cruel ones could hardly hold back their tears.
    Their hearts would burst into wails and cry:
    "God destroyed this sufferer and had no pity on him,
    Obscurity and the shadow of death seized him."

We could not believe what our ears kept hearing.
    Birds were not singing and the cocks were all sleeping.
    The lugubrious sound of the death of the innocent rose into
        Heaven.
    My eyes, my eyes stream with tears and cannot sleep.

"You, Lord, ordained this," said the good Matatron.
    Elijah the Prophet, running to and fro, asked if there were any
        rescue.
    The angels, headed by Raphael and Michael, did not speak;
    Rather they all read psalms, shed tears, and wailed.

The torturers in their anguish saw much misery and sorrow.
    Let that night be taken by darkness and not be followed by day.
    God darkened our souls and our vision.
    Mourning took hold of us as if we were corpses arisen.

Barouh Dayan Aémeth, Gouay dé mozotros ké blasfémimos i
   pékimos
Mos vino mal por el abandonno dé la Tora i por nouestros
   délitos
O Adonay, non embiès fouégo en los gouessos dé tous amantès
O DIO Piadozo, conortamos i ké séas con nosotros klémanté .

Cavalla 27 Hechvan 5702
17 Novembre 1942—Lundi

A la Memoria del mouy régrétado
Simantov Yaacov Mihaël ki foué
matado por los Bulgaros.

Blessed be the true judge.[6] Woe to us who have blasphemed and
  sinned.
Evil befell us for abandoning the Torah and for our
  transgressions.
O Lord! Do not send fire into the bones of those who love You.
O merciful God! Sustain us and be compassionate with us.

Kavalla, 27 Heshvan 5702
17 November 1942—Monday

To the memory of the sadly missed
Simantov Yaacov Mihael, who was
killed by the Bulgarians.

El primo grito en la angustia !

DIO mio ! Es esfouénio o mi meoillo non esta en mi ?
Ké réalita amarga mis ojos constatan, ké alborotamiento en mi !
Ma, ès possivlé ? Mé apalpo entéro, pronounsio médios biervos
Como créèr à la disparition totala dé los Gidios éternos siervos !

Mis ojos, mis ojos verted lagrimas abondatès i sin kédar
Las dezgrasias arivadas à mi Pouevlo non sé pouéden kontar.
El méoillo mé sé tira, sé trouvia i réfousa dé razonar
La inteligensa oumana délantré esté mal non kiéré foncsionar !

Padré kérensiozo ! Como sératès tou corason à tanta manzia !
Sératès tous ojos por non ver el révanio ké con tanta pouerkéria
Los énémigos iziéron dé eillos. I sératès à tous oillidos
Por non sentir dé tanta alma en péna los amanziantès djimidos !

O ijas dé mi Pouevlo ! Aynda ailler yénas dé vidas i alégria
Como kaillitech en mano dé matadorès à sentimientos dé
    barbaria !
Viéjos i viéjas, tchikos i tchikas, sakatès infirmos i hazinos
Como vos arankaron dé vouestras kazas por mandarvos en
    caminos !

Almas inotchentès dé mi Pouevlo, como fuetech kitados dé las
    cazas
Como formaron dé vozotros cortégios founébrès dé bivos en
    masas !
Ma, ké corason pouédé tener el ombré por azer coza séméjanté !
Povéro Israel, tous trajédias pasadas fouéron mas angoustiantès ?

The First Cry in Anguish

O my God! Is it a dream or am I out of my mind?
What bitter reality do my eyes see, what confusion within me!
But is it possible? I touch myself, I murmur half words.
How can one believe in the total disappearance of the Jews, Your
    eternal servants!

My eyes, my eyes shed abundant and never-ending tears.
The misfortunes that befell Your people cannot be counted.
My brain tears apart, my mind is troubled and refuses to reason.
Human intelligence refuses to function before this evil.

Loving Father! How could you close Your heart to such a tragedy?
You closed your eyes so as to not see the abominations that on Your
    flock
The enemy has visited. And You closed Your ears
Not to hear from so many souls in pain the lamentable moans!

O daughters of my people! Only yesterday, full of life and
    happiness,
How you fell into the hands of murderers with barbarous intent!
Old men and women, boys and girls, the lame, the infirm, and the
    sick,
How they uprooted you from your homes to send you on the
    roads!

Innocent souls of my people, how you were removed from your
    homes,
How they formed with you funereal corteges of human beings en
    masse.
What kind of a heart can man have to carry out such a deed!
Unfortunate Israel, your past tragedies, were they more sorrowful?

Patron del moundo ! Datan, Aviram i Korah pékaron despoues dé
   Sinay
I la tierra sé engloutio à todos eillos en nombré dé Adonay .
Ma à los ijos dé Korah non métitès à mouerté i déchatès en vida
Exemplo à los survivientès porké anden en la bouéna via.

Dé los yoros dé tanto dezgrasiado formando el rio fourienté
Vienen abrévarsen Samael con sous andjélès dé la mouerté !
Los énémigos sé alégraron mas dé la kaillida del Beth Amikdach
Couando como boratchos dé vino dé alégria ensansivlès saltach !

Mi corason adoloriado dezrézona, la dezgrasia ès immensa !
El entelecto oumano sé réfouza dé examinar la trensa !
La catastrofa non tiéné sou igoual en la estoria dé los Pouevlos
La amargoura dé mi alma ès sin conorté débacho dé los Ciélos !
O DIO Potenté ! lévantaté como baragan i ven salvamos !
A mozotros tous ijos sin défensa dé mouestros malès soulajamos !

Olympiada 10 Véadar 5703
17 Marso 1943—Miercolès

En la notché del 3 al 4 Marso 1943 los Bulgaros tomaron à todos
los Djidios dé Serres, Drama, Cavalla, Xanthi, Gumulgina i Dédéa-
gatch sé los yévaron en Bulgaria i dé ailli los aougaron dizen en el
Danoubio. A mi non mé tocaron. Dizid, si kiérech: MIRACOLO.

Master of the World! Dathan, Abiram, and Korah have all sinned after Sinai
And the earth swallowed all of them in Your Holy Name.
But You did not put the children of Korah to death; rather You let them live
To be an example to the living survivors to walk in the path of righteousness.

From the torrential river formed by the tears of so many unfortunate ones,
Samael and his Angels of Death come to quench their thirst.
The enemies rejoiced more from the destruction of the Beth Amigdash[7]
When, as if intoxicated by wine, they dance with wanton pleasure!

My sorrowful heart reasons irrationally; the tragedy is immense.
Human intellect refuses to examine the predicament.
The catastrophe has no equal in the history of mankind.
The bitterness of my soul is without consolation under Heaven.
O Omnipotent God! Rise up as a Champion and come to save us.
Help us, Your defenseless children; relieve our suffering.

Olympiada, 10 Veadar 5703
17 March 1943—Wednesday

On the night of March 3 and 4, 1943, the Bulgarians took all the Jews from Xeres, Drama, Kavalla, Xanthi, Cumulgina, and Dedeagatch and carried them to Bulgaria and from there to the Danube where, so they say, they drowned them. They did not catch me. You may say, if you wish: A miracle.

El segoundo grito en la angoustia !

SANTO DIO ! A mézoura ké mas en répozo mi meoillo pensa
La catastrofa arivada à mi Pouevlo aparésé mas immensa !
Milès dé almas sin défensa como codréros fouéron tomados
I al dégoillido en tierra bien londjanas fouéron yévados !

El énémigo ké dé todo tiempo vélava por daniar à Israel
Vido con alégria dé corasson al Djidio, sospirando el !
Como bestias salvajès todos eillos é rojaron al espojo
Aoutorès dé la rouvina complida del Pouevlo mio mouy
    malorozo !

La rouvina dé todos mozotros i dé los meldadorès dé la LEY
Los livros Santos razgados, trespizados con négra Fey
Ké alégria, DIO del Ciélo, estos berbantès consintiéron
Eciandosen como léonès ambrentos sovré la préa ké coumiéron !

O Criador del Moundo ! Como déchatès consoumir esté crimen !
Como permétitès tanta dezgrasia sovré los ké dizen AMEN ?
Mi méoillo sé bola dé mi cavassa por el malor dé mi rassa
El non pouédé conséver la immansita dé la dezgrassia !

Por coualo dunké déchatès consumir à tou Pouevlo por salvajès ?
Si son moutchos los pékados mouestros i dé nouestro antourajé
Délantré la mizéria i la mouerté ké entéros mos acapararon
No pouédé ser ké nouestros yoros i sangloutos non té tokaron !

The Second Cry in Anguish

Holy God! The longer my mind in repose reflects,
The catastrophe that has befallen my people appears the more
    intense.
Thousands of defenseless souls were taken like lambs
And carried off to be slaughtered in faraway lands.

The enemy who, from time immemorial, was watching to harm
    Israel
Saw with a joyful heart the Jew sigh.
Like savage beasts they all threw themselves on the spoils;
Authors of the complete destruction of my most unfortunate
    people.

The ruin of us all and of the readers of the Law—
The holy books were torn and trampled with evil intent.
What satisfaction, O Heavenly God, these evildoers felt—
Throwing themselves like hungry lions on the prey they
    devoured!

O Creator of the Universe! How could You let this crime take
    place?
How could You allow such misfortune to happen to those who
    say Amen?
My mind blows away thinking of the adversity of my people.
It cannot conceive the immensity of the tragedy!

Why then did You allow Your people to be consumed by
    barbarians?
If our sins and the sins of those around us are many,
Considering all the misery and death which completely took hold
    of us,
Is it possible that our cries and sighs did not move You?

Como démandarté grasia i piadad por todas las almas en péna ?
Como démandarté salvation por todos los sufrientès en esta
  chéna ?
Si las lagrimas amargas dé mis ojos pouédian afalagarté
Yo yoraria sin estankar toda mi vida i sin kécharmé ! !

Ah ! El énémigo aharvo subitamenté al corason dé mi Pouevlo
El dozpojo, rovo, izo malitchourias i sin mirar al Ciélo !
Los tchikos non topan mas létché en los sénos dé sous madrès
Las lagrimas dé los Djovinos caillen con las dé sous padrès !

I los mouertos kéridos eillos tambien fouéron maltratados !
El Beth Ahaya ondé répozavan tantos del DIO illuminados
Foué métido dé ariva abacho, sakajado i todo rompido
I las bestias à fatchas oumanas azian todo con roillido !

Sinistré plazer el atakarsé à mouertos inofensivos !
Estos proviene dé oun Pouevlo por dingouno défendido !
O DIO ! mi corason en pédazos non pensa ké à ti
A tou magnanimita, à tous Grandéza porké agas aserkar à ti
Estos desendientès dé tous ijos kéridos los Patriarkas
Ven salvamos por tou nombré el Grandé i por la Santa Arka ! !

Varvara 23 Véadar 5703

30 Marso 1943—Martès

  Dé Cavalla yo mé avrighi à Olympiada dé la Chaleidique. Dé
Olympiada mé foué à Stavros i dé ailli à Varvara al tépédé la mon-
tagna. Ailli vino encontrarmé mi servidéra i djountos partimos por
Salonique.

How can one ask You for compassion and pity for the souls in
   pain?
How can one ask salvation for all those who suffer in this setting?
If the bitter tears of my eyes could give You satisfaction,
I would cry without cease all the days of my life and would not
   complain.

Oh! The enemy struck suddenly at the heart of my people.
He plundered, robbed, committed crimes without regard for
   Heaven.
The children do not find milk in the breasts of their mothers.
The tears of the young fall with those of their parents.

And the beloved dead, they were also abused.
The world of the Beth Hahaya[8] in which so many rested,
   illumined by God,
Was overturned, sacked, and torn up,
And the beasts with human faces did it all with hideous roaring.

A sinister pleasure, the attack against the blameless dead
Who are the remnant of a nation with no one to defend it.
O God! My shattered heart thinks only of You,
Of Your magnanimity, and of Your greatness to draw near You
These descendants of Your beloved children, the Patriarchs.
Come, save us, for the sake of Your great name and the Holy Ark!

Varvara, 23 Veadar 5703
30 March 1943—Tuesday

From Kavalla I took refuge in Olympiada of Khalkidhiki, from
where I proceeded first to Stavros and then to the top of the mountain
in Varvara. There came to meet me my servant and together we left
for Salonika.[9]

El terzo grito en la angoustia en Salonique

Mis piézès pizan las caillès dé esta benditcha sivdad
Aynda ailler yéna dé los fidélès adeptas dé Sinay
Mis ojos non tiénen el corajé de mirar en alto
La amargoura dé mi alma ès grandé o DIO Santo ! !

Yo temblo entéro ! En mi mémoria oun tablo chéchéréanté
Sé prézenta, aziendomé ver la prospérita enfitchizanté
Dé la aglomération Djoudia dé esta amada sivdad
Ké foué yamada : Yr Vaem Béisrael por sou fieldad !

El contrasto con oy ès mouy tristé i mouy malorozo !
Ni ouna alma Djoudia non existé mas ! Es amanziozo !
Cémitério, Kehiloths, Midrachims todo souziamenté profanado
Todo lo ké ès Djidio : cazas, magazénès todo esta rovado !

Lagrimas coren dé mis ojos i mis piézès non sé détienen !
Mi fiéla Anastasia, ké dezdé venté anios mé siervé
Mé détiéné por non décharmé cailler en bacho sin conosensia
I azermé apagnar por los malos énémigos sin consssenssia !

Corajé, répétava eilla, EL DIO dé tous Santos Padrès
ké té gouadro asta oy, té va salvar non moutcho mas tadré
I arivaras bien presto salvo, à tierras mas ospitaliéras
Fouillendo dé estos énémigos mizéravlès en sous carriéras !

DIO Santo ! Kien va meldar agora la Thora abandonada ?
Aki avian moutchos groupos ké la meldavan i la pratikavan !
Kien va gouadrar el Chabath, dé répozo el Grandé dia ?
Como pouédès tou assistir en spectator à esta manzia ?

Couando kémaron el Beth Amigdach manos criminalàs
Los Coanims rojaron al Ciélo las Yavès por entrégarlas .
Aki son los ajénos ké razgaron con bourla tou Santa LEY
Yévandosen à la mouerté à todos los adeptas dé tou Fey !

The Third Cry in Anguish in Salonika

My feet walk the streets of this blessed city,
Only yesterday full of faithful adherents of Sinai.
My eyes do not have the courage to look up.
The bitterness of my soul is great, O Holy God!

I tremble all over. In my memory a troubling image
Presents itself, making me see the enticing prosperity
Of the Jewish multitude of this beloved city
That was called "Yr vaem beisrael"[10] for its fidelity.

The contrast with today is sad and sorrowful indeed.
Not one Jewish soul exists any longer. It is lamentable.
The cemetery, synagogues, houses of study all filthily profaned;
All that is Jewish—houses, stores—all were robbed.

Tears run from my eyes and my feet do not stop.
My faithful Anastasia who has served me for twenty years
Holds me up to prevent me from falling unconscious
And letting the evil enemies take me in this mental state.

"Courage," she repeated, "the God of your sainted forefathers,
Who watched over you until today, will save you in the not
       distant future
And you will soon reach a more hospitable land,
Fleeing these wretched enemies in their pursuit."

O Holy God! Who will now read the abandoned Torah?
Here there were many groups who read it and lived by it.
Who will keep the Sabbath, the great day of rest?
How can You be present as a spectator of this tragedy?

When criminal hands burned the Beth Amigdash,[11]
The High Priests threw the keys to Heaven to deliver them.
Here, it is the strangers who tore in mockery Your holy Law,
Taking away to death all the followers of Your faith!

I portanto, Tou avias prométido à mouestros avouélos
Ké mezmo en la tierra dé sous énémigos débacho los Ciélos
Séré Clémanté por eillos, mis ijos, i non los destroulliré .
En sous oras dé apreto viendré à eillos i los regmiré .

DIO del moundo, DIO del moundo ! Si tou éras ombré
Yo té iva travar à djouzgo mezmo en tou Santo nombré !
Ma non sos ombré ! I yo blasfémo ! I ké pouédo yo azer
Afouéras dé yorar dé contino, siendo you non pouédo conséver
Ké Tou mos agas ansi dépiédrer por mouestros angoustiadorès
Menten tou prometa i mandamos presto mouestros
    salvadorès ! !

ATHENA 11 Iyar 5703
16 Mayo 1943—Alhad

A mi bouen amigo DARYO LEVY

Arivi en Athéna viniendo dé Cavala i dé los kazalès dé la Chal-
eidique sin ké dingouna gouardia mé démandara kien so ! me miravan
i non mé vian!

And nevertheless, You had promised our ancestors,
Even in the land of their enemies under Heaven:
"I will be merciful unto them, my children, and I shall not
    destroy them;
In their hours of oppression I shall come to them and redeem
    them."

Lord of the Universe, Lord of the Universe! If You were a man
I would have brought You to judgment even in Your holy name!
But You are not a man and I blaspheme. And what can I do
But cry endlessly, since I cannot conceive
That You should thus have us obliterated by our oppressors.
Keep Your promise and send us our saviors quickly.

                              Athens, 11 Iyar 5703
                              16 May 1943—Sunday

To my good friend Daryo Levy.

I reached Athens from Kavalla and the villages of Khalkidhiki
without guards asking me who I was. They would look at me but
would not see me.

I a mouestro apreto . . .

Tou, Yousséf fouétes mas ventourozo ké los otros.
Couando mé anounsiaron tou mouerté con lagrimas dé yoros
Mi alma sé atristo como traversada por agoudos rayos
Ma i ouna sonriza dé contentes passo por mis lavios.

Siendo vidé ké el Dio té réservo del djousto la souerté
Por azerté répozar en tierra dé paz el té mando la mouerté
El non permetio ké tou pouerpo arastara por los campos
Prés comestivlé à las aghilas con sous dientes dé gantchos.

Tou abédigouavas i salvavas moutchas almas en soufriensa
Tou azias la Sédaka à todos con moutcha entelligensa
Dé siénès dé famiglias tou réssivias siempré bendission
Izites lo bouéno mijor ké otros ricos en tou sitouation.

El Dio via tou ovra, estava contenté i oy té récompensa.
El mouerir entré los souillos arodéado ès alégria immensa
El mouérir adientro dé sou caza ès paga dé los zahoutiéros
I tou fouétès la providensia i dé miles dé forastéros.

Hélas! Si por oy véo la paga divina ké té ès dada
Mi yoro éclata dé ouna i con fortaléza i con boz atabafada
Déchatès ô Grandé Yosseph oun grandé vazio entré mozotros
Yoros i algouilla van à endetchar dé los nouestros los otros.

En la bouraska ké esta aharvando nouestro Pouevlo
Ménazandolo aki dé dépédrission totala débacho el Ciélo
Couanto ivas à ser provétchozo à todos los rezfouillidos
Ké, por milagro, van à pouéder salvarssen del dégoillio.

Sin kérerlo, Vénérado Yosseph ayoudates à los énémigos
Tou mouerté va cavzar la mouerté dé moutchos amigos
Dé akeillos moutchos ké en las oras aprétadas actoualas
Sé mantienen en vida grassias à tous dadivas libéralas.

And To Our Misfortune . . .

You, Joseph, were more fortunate than the others.
When they informed me of your death, with tearful eyes
My soul agonized as if pierced by sharp thunderbolts.
But also a gratifying smile crossed my lips,

Realizing that God rightfully reserved for you such a fate.
To let you rest in peaceful land He caused this death.
He did not allow your body to be dragged through the camps,
Prey for eagles with hooks for teeth.

You helped and saved many souls in pain.
You gave charity to everyone with understanding.
From hundreds of families always you received blessings.
You did more good than other rich men.

God saw your deeds, was satisfied, and today rewards you.
Dying surrounded by one's family is immense happiness.
Dying in one's house is compensation for the charitable,
And you were the provider for thousands of strangers.

Alas! If today I see the Divine reward given to you,
My cry suddenly bursts forth with vigor and with a stifled voice.
You left behind, O great Joseph, a vast void among us,
And the others will mourn our people with cries and wails.

In the storm that is striking our nation,
Threatening them with total extermination,
How helpful you could have been to all the fugitives,
Who, by miracle, will be able to be saved from the slaughter.

Unintentionally, venerable Joseph, you helped our enemies.
Your death will cause the death of many friends,
Of the many who in the present gloomy hours
Stay alive because of your generous gifts.

O Dio del Ciélo! Té démando por coualo mos aharvas tanto
Atorgamos somos pékadorès ma somos tous ijos portanto
Somos esseres oumanos ké sigoun ti criados à tou imajé
Non mos rendimos coulpantes dé actos inoumanès i salvajès.

Mos déchatès como oun révanio abandonado i sin pastor
Délantré péricolos mortalès i dé oun énémigo aravdonados
Préa fatchilé à los lovos oumanos coudouzès i crourélès
Ké sé estan vengando dé todos mozotros tous ijos fiélès
Nada ké por nouestra flakéza mérésémos ser sostouvidos
Salvamos à mozotros tous ijos endjoustamenté aboréssidos.

Athéna Tichri 5.704
Octobre 1943

O Heavenly God! I ask why You beat us so.
We admit we are sinners; still, we are Your children.
We are human beings, as You stated, created in Your image.
We are not guilty of inhuman and savage acts.

You deserted us like a flock abandoned and without a shepherd,
Facing mortal dangers and savagely treated by an enemy,
An easy prey to ravening and cruel human wolves
Who are taking vengeance on us, Your faithful children.
If only for our weakness, we deserve to be saved.
Save us, Your children, unjustly despised.

Athens, Tishri 5704
October 1943

Hanouka 5704

Sovré las rouvinas dé todos los biénés dé mi Pouevlo
Sé assentaron los énémigos i cantaron sin yélo
Eillos rovaron todo nouestro aver i sé enrékisiéron ,
I los Djidios deznoudos i croudos sé estréméssiéron .

Triomphos dé djélatès crouélès contra nanicos !
Triomphos dé léonès ambrientos contra ratonicos !
Triomphos dé fouertès i potentès contra flacos !
Triomphos dé baraganès armados contra dézarmados !

O dolor ! O ijos kéridos dé Israel persécoutido !
Como kédach gouadrados londgé dé la vista del énémigo.
Temblando entéros vos vach coumiendo las ounias
La cavessa abocada como caminando bacho las louvias !

Cada dia van aférando i sokestrando nouestros biénès
Los entrégadorès son moutchos i sé contan à siénès.
Nouestras rézervas dé dia en dia sé van apocando
Como Dio Santo azer fasès à los menestéres augmantando!

Louz ? Non sé vé. El énémigo paréssé aynda potenté
Los salvadorès tadran à venir. Eillos ya son fouertès
Ma el Dio non dicho aynda ya basta tanta angoustia
I solo en el, en sou salvation va toda nouestra féouzia.

Es ké Dio Santo, kédarémos bivos i sanos i salvos ?
Es ké el énémigo non mos aférara con sou mano dé clavos ?
Es ké las louzès dé Hanouka non mos aréloumbraran mas ?
Es ké Dio Rahman nouestras bocas non té alavaran mas ?

Asta couando Dio clémanté, conténouaré dé estar djimiendo ?
Asta couando por los malorès dé mi Pouevlo iré soufriendo ?
Asta couando toda mi cavessa sera oun dépozito dé agoua
I mis ojos fouentès courientès dé lagrimas bien amargas ?

Hanukah 5704

On the ruins of all the wealth of my people
Sat the enemies and sang in cold blood.
They stole all our possessions and got rich,
And the naked and raw Jews trembled.

Triumphs of cruel giants against midgets!
Triumphs of hungry lions against little mice!
Triumphs of the strong and mighty against the weak!
Triumphs of armed ruffians against the unarmed!

O pain! O beloved children of persecuted Israel!
How you remain in hiding out of sight of the enemy!
Trembling, you bite your fingernails,
Your heads bowed as if you were walking in the rain!

Each day they are seizing and confiscating our wealth;
The informers are many and can be counted in the hundreds.
Our reserves from day to day are diminishing.
How can you, Holy God, prosper by increasing our needs?

Light? There is none. The enemy still appears powerful;
The deliverers delay in coming. They are already strong,
But God has yet to say: "Enough of this anguish."
In Him alone, in His salvation rests our felicity.

Could it be, Holy God, that we will remain alive, safe, and sound?
Could it be that the enemy will not seize us with his fist of iron?
Could it be that the candles of Hanukah will no longer shine
    upon us?
Could it be, merciful God, that our lips will no longer praise You?

How long, compassionate God, will I go on lamenting?
How long the tribulations of my people will I suffer?
How long will my head be a cistern of water
And my eyes running springs of bitter tears?

O benditchos tiempos dé folgoura i paz révénid à mozotros
Dizid à los démonios: Atras, non ay mas lougar para vozotros
Dizid à los cativados: Rétornad con alégria à vouestras cazas
Alondjad vouestros souspiros i limounios, i vouestras ansias.

O louzès santas dé Hanouka symbolo dé espéransas para Israel
Réloumbrad nouestros destinos i ké mos protéjé Mihael
Reloumbrad los caminos, del Dio alto los ijos benditchos
Intchidnos dé confiensa como lo izitech por Hasmonay i sus ijos
Conortad, conortad nouestras almas ké estan moutcho sofriendo
Etchad en eillas el balsamo consolador i aribividor en
   bendiziendo.—

Athéna 25 Kislev 5704

22 Décembre 1943—Miercolès

A los Djidios dé Athéna

O blessed times of comfort and peace, return to us!
Tell the demons: "Go back, there is no room for you."
Tell those in distress: "Return in happiness to your homes,
Discard your sighs and groanings, and all your anxieties."

O blessed lights of Hanukah, symbol of hope for Israel,
Illumine our destiny and may Michael protect us,
Illumine the path of God's blessed children,
Fill us with confidence as you have Hasmonay[12] and his children,
Soothe, soothe our souls that are greatly suffering,
And in Your blessing anoint them with the consoling and life-
    giving balm.

Athens 25 Kislev 5704
22 December 1943—Wednesday

To the Jews of Athens

En la dolor de la ora

Mez dé Iloul, el mez dé rahamim, el mez dé piadadès
La gherra conténoua, i el ombré yéno dé maldadès
Destrouillé i mata existensias oumanas i inotchentes
La sangré corré moutcho i los criminalès kédan insolentes.

Va, povéro Pouevlo mio. El pouevlo del Dio escojido
Tou vez à tous kéridos mouertos con corasson aflijido
Té estas apourando, mouriendo en el cativério témérozo
Mouérété sin kécharté ô martério noble i mouy doloriozo!

Santo Dio! Kété izimos ké té aravias i ansi mos castigas
Répéto: Somos al igoual dé los otros pouevlos ké ké digas
A estos oultimos non los déracinas los azès sofrir solamenté
Ma à mozotros mos azes dépedrer djountos i entéramenté!

Tou, izites contrato con mozotros porké té servamos
Té aravias porké non ovédésémos i dé el mos dezviamos
Ma, esté contrato ès tou ké lo izitès con tou Djenté
I por esto dévias mostrarté siempre mas indoulgenté;

Mos trailles en grado dé dizirté malgrado mozotros
Ké ya mos esvatchéamos dé ser tous ijos amanziozos
Manco ser " Mamlehet coanims vé goy kadoch" i yorar
Toma à otros Pouevlos i sanctificalos en nouestro lougar.

Dio del moundo! Es ké kijimos nozotros nasser Djidios
Couando la fatalita, nouestra vinida al moundo décidio?
Lo savès mouy bien: Es ké kijimos nasser del todo?
Non mos démandaron nouestro avizo en dingoun dé los modos,

In the Agony of Time

The month of Elul, the month of mercy, the month of
    compassion.
The war continuous, and man, abounding in evil,
Destroys and kills human and innocent beings.
Blood overflows and the criminals remain insolent.

Go, my unfortunate people, the nation that God chose.
You see our beloved dead with a sorrowful heart.
You are consuming yourself, dying in a frightful captivity.
Die without complaining, O noble and pitiful martyrs!

Holy God! What have we done to You for Your wrath and
    punishment?
I repeat: We are equal to other peoples, what have You to say?
Them you do not uproot, You only make them suffer;
But us, You destroy altogether and completely.

You made a covenant with us to serve You.
You become angry because we do not obey and from Your ways
    we deviate.
But this covenant—You made it with Your people,
And for that reason, You should show Yourself always more
    indulgent.

You have brought us to the point of telling You in spite of
    ourselves
That we are weary of being Your pitiful children.
Short of being "Mamhelet coanim ve goy kadoch,"[13] and we cry,
Take other peoples and sanctify them in our stead.

God of the Universe! Is it that we wanted to be born Jews,
When fate decided our coming into the world?
You know it well: Is it that we wanted to be born?
No one, in any way or manner, asked for our advice.

Por esto dévias meter en el ombré sentimientos piadozos
Dévias kitar dé sou sangré los instinctos péricolozos
Dévias meter en sou alma amor, compassion, paz i bouendad
I ké sou corasson non conosiéra ké solo la dérétchédad.

Por contra el ombré ès el mas férotché dé los animalès
El fouerté sé ataka al flaco con modos todo criminalès
I ké dizir dé nozotros Pouevlo tchiko i sin défensa
Ké énémigos crouélès i bachos mos kitan toda fouerssa !

Dio del Moundo! Mira si ay dolor como nouestra dolor!
Mira si ay otras nasionès ké souffren del mezmo malor
Eillas sé rien i sé bourlan, yo los vidé, sin trégoua
Gritti : I sovré vozotros va passar el vazo dé la adefla!
Ven Dio aynda ès tiempo porké salvès à los povéros cativos
Protéjamos i castiga dé las otras Nationès à los malinos.

ATHENA 1 Illoul 5704
20 Agosto 1944—Alhad

For this reason You should have given man a compassionate
    nature.
You should have removed from his blood the dangerous instincts.
You should have placed in his soul love, compassion, peace, and
    goodness,
And his heart should only have known justice.

On the contrary, man is the most ferocious of all animals;
The strong attacks the weak in the most criminal ways.
And what can one say of us, a few defenseless people,
From whom cruel and perverse enemies take away all strength.

God of the Universe! See if there is a greater pain than ours!
See if other nations suffer the same misfortune.
I have seen them laugh and ridicule without pause.
I cried out: "To you shall pass the bitter cup."
Come, God, there is still time to save the wretched captives.
Protect us and punish the wicked ones of other nations.

Athens, 1 Elul 5704
20 August 1944—Sunday

Oun poco de louz

La sitouation viéné dé trocar. El malditcho énémigo partio
Los Inglézès viniéron, la mourailla del esclavajé caillo
Despoues dé contrailler tanto mal à los ombrès i à la monéda
Los Almanès dé sous propia volontad abandonaron Athéna.

Las manifestasionès sé sigouien alégrès i toumoultouozas
La grandé massa dé la popoulation con boukétos dé rozas
Abachan en las plassas con modos dé bandiéras i oriflamas
Dezbordando dé gozo i alégria proviniendo dé sous almas.

Desdé el primer dia yo empessi à encontrar dé los mios
Saliendo dé sous escondidijos con attentivos acavidos
Dando loorès al Criador todo Pontenté, por esté milagro
Non sé sienté dingoun tono ni dizcordanté ni agro.

En grandé Keyla ouna orasion dé alégria ès organizada
Todos à ouna kiéren alavar al Dio en esta bouéna sémanada
Eillos cantan en djountos todos los salmos dé alégria
Mourmouréados por los assistientès en toda compagnia.—

En soupétas los sonès del Chofar sentir sé iziéron
Al primo toutouroutoutou los corassonès sé dezliéron
Ménéo las almas dé todos los ombrès i las moujérès
Ké tétéréaron como nounca en sous profondos essérès.—

La comossion ressentida foué mouy grandé i fouerté
Los sonès del chofar paressian espander sonès dé mouerté
El aver i las parédés mezmo dé esta caza dé orassion
Retenblavan como mozotros, aférados dé santa émosion.

Todos, tchikos i grandès sé récojéron en si temblando
Non sé descrivé lo ké sous almas ressentian en tétéréando
Los ojos sé empagnaron i las lagrimas abondantès cailleron
Lagrimas santas entré las santas como coual nounca ouviéron

A Little Hope

The situation has just changed. The accursed enemy left.
The British came; the wall of slavery fell.
After causing much misery to all men and taking their wealth,
The Germans abandoned Athens of their own free will.

Happy, tumultuous parades keep taking place.
The great mass of the population, with bouquets of roses
Descends on the squares with all types of flags and banners,
Overflowing with joy and happiness arising from their souls.

From the first day I began to find my people
Leaving their hiding places with guarded care,
Giving praise to the Omnipotent Creator for this miracle;
Not a discordant or sour note is heard.

In the main synagogue a joyful prayer is organized.
All, in unison, want to praise God in this blessed week.
They sing together all the happy psalms,
Murmured in unison by those in attendance.

Suddenly the sound of the shofar was heard.
On the first blast all hearts stood still;
It moved the souls of all the men and women,
Who trembled as never before in their innermost hearts.

The agitation they experienced was very great and strong;
The sounds of the shofar seemed to spread funereal wails.
The atmosphere, even the walls of this house of prayer,
Trembled as we did, seized with the feeling of holiness.

Everyone, young and old, withdrew within himself, trembling;
One cannot describe what their shivering souls felt.
The eyes became blurred and many tears fell;
Holiest of holy tears such as never were before.

Ma, la sitouation dé los salvados dé oy ès bien trajika
Dé 90.000 Djidios dé esté Paèz los 85.000 azen faltida
Dio del Ciélo ! Dé todas las bocas salé la mezma coza :
Espavoréssienté estado i trajédia oultra téméroza !

Kien foué rovado con sous biénés i entrégado à los Almanès
Kien despoues dé dezvalizado fouillo à los andartès
Kien ménazado por ké diéra todos sous biénés i sous aver
Kien livrado à los óunos con prometta dé kitarlos del Paèz!

En sous profondos escondidijos todos djémian i yoravan.
Démandavan aillouda del Eternel, à las cailladas rogavan.
Salvation dé poder del énémigo dé adientro i dé afouéra
El corasson sé dezpédassa, Dio mio, ansi ké non fouéra.

Cajé todos salimos deznoudos i croudos i bien hazinos
Estamos sin mézos dé existenssia en poder dé malinos
Non kiéren rétornarmos nouestras groutas i nouestras cazas
Non ay kien sé apiadé i corra por nouestras cavzas !

I esté tablo tambien dezparessé complidamenté
El pensério dé los yévados en cativério dezgrasiadamenté
Sé prézenta à nouestra vista i estrindjé nouestra alma
Mos azé oulvidar todo pensando ounicamenté à sous cavza.

I las lagrimas dé estos salvados dé oy dé mouévo caillen
Dé sous boccas aviertas ni oun biervo, solo souspiros salen
I portanto à moutchos dé los prézentès, con affliction
Yo mezmo les avia prévédido esta maloroza persécoution.

Les avia conséjado con amor dé yrsen en Eretz Israel
Dé instalarsen i servir el Paez con dévouamiento fièl
Assegourandossen sous salvation i la dé toda sou Djenté
Egoyzmo altanto ménestérozo por las oras solamenté.—

However, the situation of those safe today is really tragic.
Of ninety thousand Jews of this country, eighty-five thousand are
    missing.
God in Heaven! From every lip is uttered the same
Frightening state and tragedy beyond all terror!

Some were robbed of their wealth and denounced to the Germans;
Some, after being abandoned, took refuge in attics;
Some were threatened to make them surrender all their riches
    and possessions,
Some were handed to the Ounos with the promise of being sent
    out of the country.

In their deep hiding places they moaned and cried.
They asked assistance from God and prayed quietly
For deliverance from the yoke of foreign and domestic enemies.
The heart breaks, O God! O that this never had happened!

Almost all of us emerged naked and raw and very sick.
We are in the hands of cruel people with no means of survival;
No one wants to return our stores and our homes;
There is no one to take pity on us and fight for our cause.

Even this panorama disappears completely.
The thought of the deported in captivity unfortunately
Presents itself to our view and grips our soul.
It makes us forget everything because we think only of its cause.

And the tears of those who are safe today fall once again;
From their open mouths not a word is uttered, only sighs.
And I, however, to many of those present, with grief
Had personally predicted this disastrous persecution.

With love I had advised them to go to Eretz Israel,[14]
To settle and serve the country with faithful devotion,
Assuring themselves of their salvation and that of all their people.
That degree of selfishness was necessary for those times.

Mouy pocos sintiéron. Los otros kédaron indéférentès
I la dezgrassia vino , mos toco i mos aharvo profondamenté
Ké al ménos la lission sierva i lo ké non sé izo dé antès
Sé aga agora presto i tornen à Sion todos sous amantès !

ATHENA 28 Tichri 5705

15 Octobre 1944—Alhad

Al amigo dé idéal Roberto Raphael

Few listened. The rest remained indifferent.
And the disaster came; it touched us and hit us deeply.
At least, let the lesson be useful, and what was not done before,
Let it be done immediately and all the faithful return to Zion.

Athens, 28 Tishri 5705
15 October 1944—Sunday

To my friend Roberto Raphael

Ticha Beav 5.704

Malor por mi! malor por mi pouevlo Israel !
En ké tristé fin trouchitès á mozotros o Eternel !
Santa Chehina, tou ké mos acompagnas dezdé anios
Porké non mos protéjas i mos espandes tous manos ?

Ke pudimos azer por meresser castighérios séméjantès ?
Non créo ké las otras Nasionès son mas entérésantès
Por coualo alora ké séa sovré nouestras cavessas solo
Ké cayga todo el mal matandomos sovre el colpo !

El énémigo aki dezdé Nissan mos aharvo mortalmenté
Todas las idadès dé ombrès i moujérès dezgrasiadamenté
Todos fouéron aférados como los péorès malazédorès
Fouéron mandados à mouerir i en négras conditionnis.

Entassados en vagonès dé bestias moy bien sérados
Ambrentos i sékéozos en las mas négra paillida aférados
Couantos dé eillos ya mouérérian de sed i asficsia
I couantos otros dé mérak dé sous almas dé apopléxia!

Les refouzaron el ayoudo dado en cavzos séméjantès
A otros dé los ajénos en estados manco amanziantès.
Tratandossé dé Djidio, nada non toca à dingouno
Todos sé alégran si dé mozotros manca mezmo ouno !

Yo kédi en esta sivdad entéra amargo i assolado
Por ver ouna fatcha dé Djidio mi corasson esta dézolado
Mi émossion ès entenssa. Kiéro yorar ma non pouédo!
Dolor mé toma al pensar la rouvina dé mi Pouevlo !

Passi por las gouardias dé las sivdadès i los Bulgaros
A las frontiéras mé décharon passar foumando cigaros
Los Allemanès viniéron asta mi cama i mé miraron
Ma el Criador mé escoundio i sous ojos sé siégaron.

Tisha Beav 5704[15]

Woe is me! Woe is my people Israel!
To what a sad end You have brought us, O Eternal God!
Holy Shekinah, You have accompanied us for years,
Why don't You protect us and spread Your hands over us?

What could we have done to merit such punishments?
I do not believe that the other nations are more pleasing.
Why, then, should there fall only upon our heads
All the misfortunes that are killing us with one blow?

The enemy here since Nisan beat us mortally,
Men and women of all ages, woefully,
They were all seized as if they were the worst wrongdoers;
They were sent to their death and in miserable conditions:

Stuffed in tightly closed cattle wagons,
Hungry and thirsty, caught up in the worst trap.
How many of them had already died of thirst and asphyxiation,
And how many more of depression in apoplexy of their own
    souls!

They were refused the help that is accorded in similar cases
To other peoples in states much less pitiful.
For the Jew no one is moved.
All are happy if even one from among us is missing.

I remained in this entire city saddened and isolated.
To see a single Jewish face my heart feels disconsolate;
My emotions are intense. I want to weep but I cannot;
I am seized with pain when I think of the destruction of my
    people!

I passed by the guards in the cities, and the Bulgarians
At the frontiers smoking cigars let me cross.
The Germans came up to my bed and saw me,
But the Creator hid me and their eyes were blinded.

Passi alado los Italianos i los Grégos i non mé vieron
Ké yo kédara bivo i libéro ansi dé los Ciélos kijéron
Testimonio bivo por ver de la Thora las prédictionès
I los ménazos del Eternel yénos dé maldisionès !

Mis ojos kieren sérarssen à la louz del dia !
Couanto yo non existir, estar mouerto dézéaria.
Mi corasson esta yéno dé dézespéro inéfasavlé
Yo souffro como non otro i mi alma ès inconsolavlé.

Dé todos tous dezcorsos Yéchahya el Grandé Proféta
I dé todos tous conortès O Yermia, véo solo prometas
El pessimismo préto mio mé poucha à todo blasfémar
Ironia amarga ké mé azé pensar à kierer todo rouvinar:

Si el sol sé amata para siempré i non mos caillenta mas
I si la Louna clara sé escouréssé dé mas en mas
I si los pacharos para siempré kédaran dé djoundjouléar
I si dé las rozas non sé pouedra mas sous gouezmos respirar

I si los arvolès non créséran ni ermoyésséran mas
I si todo modo dé planta non sé rénovélara nounca mas
I si los Gayos non cantaran al amanesser i al anotchesser
I si péchès dé la mar non saltaran mas al esclaresser

I si el rossio la maniana non couvrira mas nada
I si el imbat o zéphir non soplara mas las manianadas
I si conténouara à cailler louvia dé achouffré i dé fouégo
I si toda alma biva séra destroullida por el trouéno

I si toda la tierra sé va azer ouna immensa tomba
Por engloutirsé à todo modo dé criado i sou solombra
I si el Tocu vavoou va a reynar dé mouévo sovré la création
I si nada non va aprésourar dé traermos la salvation

I passed near the Italians and the Greeks and they did not see me.
For me to stay alive and free, this was the wish of Heaven;
To be a living testimony of the prophecies of the Torah
And of God's warnings, which abound with damnations.

My eyes want to block out the light of day;
How I long not to live; to be dead is my wish.
My heart is full of unforgettable despair;
I suffer as no one else and my soul is inconsolable.

Of all your utterances, great Prophet Isaiah,
And of all your soothings, O Jeremiah, I only see promises.
My dark pessimism presses me to blaspheme;
Bitter irony that causes me to think of destroying everything:

If the sun would go out forever and would not warm us,
And if the clear moon would darken more and more,
And if the birds would forever stop singing,
And if the scent of the flowers would no longer give perfume,

And if the trees would no longer grow and beautify the land,
And if all types of plants would not renew themselves,
And if the cocks would not crow at dawn or at nightfall,
And if the fish in the sea would not jump at daybreak,

And if the morning dew would not cover the land,
And if the imbat[16] and zephyr[17] would no longer blow in the
    mornings,
And if the rain of stones and fire would continue to fall,
And if all living creatures would be destroyed by thunder,

And if all the Earth would become an immense grave
To swallow all created species and their shadow,
And if the original chaos would reign anew over all Creation,
And if nothing would hasten to bring us salvation,

I tanto ké Samael i Achméday sé rièn dé mouestro mal yévar
I tanto ké Matatron i los andjélès non azen otro ké yorar
Ké mé emporta, Dio Santo, visto el estado dé mi Pouevlo
Estado kajé éterno el mas péor sovré todo el souelo
Ondé non reyno i non reyna ké el déritto del mas fouerté
Ké mé emporta, Dio Eternel, o la vida o la mouerté !

ATHENA 9 AV 5.704

Al amigo ISAAC BENROUBI

And as long as Samael and Asmodeus laugh at our suffering,
And as long as Matatron and the Angels do nothing but cry,
What do I care, Holy God, in view of the condition of my people,
An almost eternal situation, the worst on all the Earth,
Where never reigned and never shall reign but the right of the
    strong,
What do I care, Eternal God, whether I live or die?

Athens, 9 Av 5704

To my friend Isaac Benroubi

Despoues de la catastrofa en Salonique

Como en oun fiéro tan souzio el oro pouro sé troco !
Como en oun sembolo ajéno el nouestro sé abolto !
Como en esta bouéna localita yamada Yr Vaèm béisrael
Todo dévino ajéno i non sé sienté mas nombrar Asael !

Camino por las caillès dé esta benditcha sivdad
Malgrado el sol todo mé paréssé estar en la escouridad
Mi fatcha dé afouéra amostra alégré ma mi ojo lagriméa
Mi alma mas ké tristé ver todo Djidios eilla dézéa.—

Por contra dé mis dos lavios arésécados i temblantès
Salen emprécasionès i biervos dé émosion poco consolantès
para ouna alma ké ressienté los malorès dé sou Pouevlo,
Dé esté Pouevlo innocenté entré otros débacho el Ciélo!

I sin kiérerlo yo mourmouréy, mis ojos verso el Eternel:
" Ansi empésso sou endétcha Iyov por el i por Israel
" Sé dépédriéra entéro el dia ké foué nassido en el
" I la notché ké sé dicho ensentada dé varon como el!

" Akeilla notché fouéra escouridad i la tomara la mouerté
" Non la rékijera el Dio dé ariva por sou négra souerté
" I non esclaréssiéra sovré eilla mas ni louz ni claridad
" La arodéaran las tiniévlas i non la viéra la oumanidad"!

Mé aresti. Vidé al profesor Mihael Molho arestarssé
Mé dio la mano: Salvimos Zéhout Avoth mé dizé sin cansarsé
Mé kédi caillado. El sanglouto sé afogava en mi garganta
Mé empédia dé pronounsiar mezmo ouna palavra clara i santa.

After the Catastrophe in Salonika

How into rusted iron pure gold has been transmuted!
How our character has been changed into a foreign one!
How, in this great city called Yr Vaem beisrael
Everything became alien and one no longer hears the name Asael!

I walked along the streets of this blessed city.
In spite of the sun it all seems dark.
My face appears to be happy, but my eyes shed tears.
My soul, more than sad, yearns to see a Jew.

On the contrary, from my lips, dry and trembling,
Surge curses and passionate words, hardly comforting
To a person who suffers the misfortunes of his people,
Of this people, of all the Earth's nations the most innocent.

And without wanting to, I murmured, my eyes lifted toward God.
Thus Job began his dirge for himself and for Israel:
"Would that the day on which I was born had utterly vanished
As well as the night in which it was said, 'Of a male she is
    pregnant'!

"Would that this night had been dark and been taken away by
    Death,
And, because of its evil fate, would that God in Heaven had not
    summoned it,
And would that neither light nor hope had dawned on it;
Would that darkness had encircled it and no human had seen it!"

I stopped. I saw Professor Michael Molho stop.
He shook my hand. "We are safe Zehout Avoth,"[18] he told me
    again and again.
I kept silent. The sob caught in my throat
And prevented me from uttering even one clear and holy word.

Yo enditchi la catastrofa. La vidé ké con toda prissa coria
Kien va endétchar agora la disparission dé esta Djoudéria
Kien va azer réssalir la piédrita colossola i tan grandémenté
Ké el Dio mos enflijo en dépiedriendomos cajé entéramenté

I yo avagar mé alondjo abatido con la cavessa abocada
Kiéro caminar con firméza i tener mi alma résignada
Non kiéro yorar, kéro ser endéférenté ma non lo pouédo
Son grandès i mé tocan moutcho los malorès dé mi Pouevlo.—

Véo: Cortéjos dé bivos en massas, en tassados en vagonès
De bestias bien entézo, sérados i siados como los mélonès
Traillidos en los founebrès i malditchos lougarès dé éxécution
Los Viéjos i infirmos métidos immédiatamenté à condanation !

Despoues i los Djovinos mandados à los banios por lavarsen
Asfiksiados en bloco sin pouéder mas nounca lévantarssen
Etchados, rondjados en los Krématorios sinistrès i témérozos
Ailli dezparissieron dé mi Pouevlo los Djidios mouy noumérozos!

Trajédia como couala non ouvo nounca en el moundo
El pensar à esto escouréssé mi vista en oun solo pounto
Mis lagrimas caillen, mi yoro ès dé oun ombré onesto
Mé fouygo presto escoundiendo mi dolor en mi mezmo !

Salonique 29 AV 5705

8 Agosto 1945—Miercoles

Al professor MIHAEL MOLHO

I mourned the catastrophe. I saw that it spread with all haste.
Who is going to mourn now the disappearance of these Jews?
Who is going to proclaim the colossal and great loss,
The total extinction that God inflicted upon us?

And I slowly walk away, beaten, my head bowed.
I want to walk firmly and have my soul resigned.
I do not want to cry. I want to be indifferent, but I cannot—
The misfortunes of my people are many and touch me deeply!

I see corteges of human beings, en masse, herded into wagons
Of animals, frozen, closed, and sealed like melons,
Brought to the funereal and cursed places of execution,
The aged and sick condemned on the spot.

Afterward also the young, sent to the baths to wash,
Asphyxiated all together, unable ever to rise again,
Then thrown, pushed into the sinister and dreadful crematoria;
There vanished from my people a great number of Jews!

A tragedy such as this has never happened before in the world!
At the thought of this, my vision darkens at once.
My tears fall; my cry is that of a decent man.
I run away quickly, hiding my pain within myself.

Salonika 29 Av 5705
8 August 1945—Wednesday

To Professor Michael Molho

AVNER PERETS

A sixth-generation Israeli, Avner Perets was born in Jerusalem in 1942. All the family members who remained in Salonika were exterminated in the death camps. Perets is the director of a computer company and teaches at the Hadassa College in Jerusalem. In his spare time he writes in Hebrew and translates English children's poetry. He told me: "The literary creation in Yiddish, the language of those millions who were killed and burned in Eastern Europe, immortalizes the dead and the survivors, and stands as a monument to their memory. My wish is that the Judeo-Spanish language also accomplish the same role regarding the shuddering fate of our people [the Sephardim] in the Holocaust. . . . I have never been in Salonika, but realizing that old Jewish Salonika is my city, I cry for her fate as if I were one of her children." The poems "Siniza i fumo" (Ash and smoke) and "Echados adientro del fuego" (Cast into the fire) appeared in *Akí Yerushalayim* (no. 21, year 6, April 1984, pp. 25–27) and are reproduced here with his permission and that of Moshe Shaul, the editor of the series. A booklet entitled *Siniza i fumo* (Jerusalem: Edision bilingue) appeared in 1986 with fourteen poems in Judeo-Spanish and Hebrew concerning the Holocaust. Among them we find the two included in this volume.

Siniza i fumo

A la memoria de Saloniko—
mi esfuyenyo i mi amor

Siniza i fumo
Bolando, kayendo
En un esfuenyo malo
Sin salvasion.

En la guerta kemada
Asentada la fija
Pasharos pretos
Apretan su korason.

Siniza i fumo
Inchen sus ojos
No ay ken ke la desperte
A darle konsolasion.

Por los sielos, ariva
Pasa la luna
Tapando su kara
Kon una nuve—karvon.

Ash and Smoke

To the memory of Salonika—
My dream and my love

Ash and smoke
Flying, falling
Into a nightmare
Without rescue.

In the parched garden
The girl sits;
Black birds
Tear at her heart.

Ash and smoke
Fill her eyes;
There is no one to wake her,
To comfort her.

In the sky above
The moon passes,
Hiding her face
In a cloud of ashes.

Echados adientro del fuego

Echados adientro
de un forno
de fuego ensendido.
Ken es el Dio
ke vos eskapara
del fuego ensendido?

Ansiano de dias—
Vuestro Dio ke servitesh
en siglos de oro,
en siglos de eskuridad—
no vos eskapara
del fuego ensendido.

Malahe a-sharet abashan
de los altos sielos
A akompanyar kon alas arankadas
los kuerpos destruidos
i entregarsen kon eyos
al fuego kemante.

I el ansiano de dias
kedara kayado.

Cast into the Fire

Cast into
an oven
of catching fire.
Who is the God
that will save you
from the catching fire?

Ancient of Days[19]—
Your god whom you served
in centuries of gold,
in centuries of darkness,
will not save you
from the catching fire.

The Malahe a-sharet[20] descend
from the heavens above
to accompany with their rent wings
the destroyed bodies
and to deliver themselves with them
into the burning fire.

And the Ancient of Days
will remain silent.

CHELOMO REUVEN

Born in Salonika, Chelomo Reuven received his primary education in French and while still a student began to publish poetry and prose articles in Judeo-Spanish and French, by demand, in the most prestigious newspapers, including *La Action, El Messagero,* and *La Verdad.* He also published poems in French using the pseudonym Le Reveur Solitaire. Upon finishing his studies, Reuven took an active part in the Zionist movement as the director of Bethar, a youth organization, and was the editor of the Zionist papers *La Nasyon* and *La Boz Sionista.* He is the author of a musical, *Esther,* and a play, *Amor por la tierra;* his literary accomplishments include a novel, *Bacho el sielo blu de oriente encantador* (Under the blue sky of the enchanting Levant), and a study entitled *La calomnia de la sangre a traverso la estoria* (Blood libels throughout history). In 1935 he moved to Israel, where he continued writing and lecturing on national themes and on the Holocaust, becoming one of the leaders of the Greek community and president of the Association de Amistad Israel-Hellas. "The Holocaust was the cause of the death of my mother, my sister and two brothers and their eight children," he told me. "Sixty thousand Jews of Salonika and other Greek cities also perished." This tragic chapter in the Diaspora continued to influence this journalist and poet, who dedicated all his efforts to the Centre de Recherches sur le Judaisme de Salonika. The poems appearing here were published in Judeo-Spanish newspapers in Israel.

Yom Hachoa

A la memoria de mi madre i de todos
mis keridos desparesidos en Aushwitz.

. . . I ke pasen los anios, ke emblankeska la kavesa,
ke los ojos se empanien i ke temblemos al kaminar,
nunka puedremos ulvidar akeya dolor espessa
de ver un puevlo entero al degoyio kondanar.

Sin kura es la yaga porke grande la trajedia,
se sekaron mas las lagrimas i no estanka la dolor,
Pasa el dia, viene la notche i espunta un nuevo dia
sin ke akaye mi djimido, sin ke konsienta mi malor.

Eyos me vienen vijitar en mi esfuenio kada notche,
ombres, mujeres, kriaturas, todos guiados por los tchesmes
de bestias armadas fin los dientes . . . i un grito atrotche
salta de mi petchadura i viene romper la kayades.

Skeletos bivos entre los kualos se distinguen mis keridos,
madre, ermanos kon sus ijos, ermana, andando en la kalmedad
de un vasto nekrotafio, komo sakrifisios ofridos
a un Moloch deskonosido, baniando en su krueldad.

Eyos yevan sovre sus ombros el pezgo de sus kativerio,
sus miradas son si vida i flaka sus respirasion
Eyos konsienten ke estos kampos seran un vasto semiterio
onde fin poko reynara una profonda dezolasion.

Aushwitz, Trablinka, Maydanik, deskonosidos lugares
ke devinieron en un dia simbolos de bestialidad,
ke arankaron miliones de almas de sus kayentes ogares
i trokaron en vanos biervos kultura i humanidad.

En rendimiento yeno ovraron los krematorios,
foyas imensas fueron kuviertas de kadavres i de kal,
i la sangre judia kurio, kayente i a tchoros
Vazieada por un puevlo asasino ke no avra otro komo tal.

Yom Hachoa[21]

To the memory of my mother and all
my dear ones who disappeared in Auschwitz.

... And the years pass, and the hair turns gray,
and the eyes dim, and we tremble when we walk;
we can never forget that heavy pain
of seeing an entire nation condemned to the slaughter.

Incurable is the wound because great is the tragedy;
the tears have dried and the pain does not cease.
The day passes, the night comes, and a new day dawns
without suppressing my moans, without my accepting my
    misfortune.

They come to visit me in my sleep every night:
men, women, children, all guided by the top boots
of beasts armed to the teeth ... and an atrocious scream
emerges from my breast and breaks the silence.

Living skeletons, among whom are my dear ones, can be seen,
mother, brothers with their children, sister, walking in the
    tranquility
of a vast necropolis, sacrifices offered
to an unknown Moloch, bathing in his cruelty.

They carry on their shoulders the weight of their bondage;
their faces are lifeless and their breathing weak.
They sense that these camps will be a vast cemetery
where soon will reign a profound desolation.

Auschwitz, Treblinka, Maidanek, unknown places
that became overnight symbols of bestiality,
that uprooted millions of souls from their warm homes
and changed into empty words culture and humanity.

For abundance operated the crematoria,
vast trenches were covered with cadavers and lime,
and the Jewish blood ran, warm and gushing,
emptied by an assassin nation that will never be equaled.

I kontinuan a andar ombres, mujeres i kriaturas
verso sus triste destino, verso las kamaras a gaz.
Eyos konsienten de avanso las horivles torturas
ke los esperan, i sus riflo no se konsiente mas.

Pokos puntos . . . i de los ornos suve una godra nuve
griza, en flama, i espande una fuerte golor
i la tierra no tembla, la natura no se ezmove
i los sielos no se estremesen de una djusta folor.

Ansi disparissieron sech miliones de ermanos.
La hydra a las mil unias los englutio sin piadad,
el asasino izo su ovra i el puevlo de los germanos
—komo si no era kulpavle—goza oy de su libertad.

El mundo entero asistio al spektakolo makabre
sin ke perkure de salvar, de ayudar, de kastigar,
sin ke sea ezmovido por todo un puevlo-kadavre
sin ke menos aga prova de repintirse o de niegar.

Ma sovre los kampos de muerte i de akeya nuve griza
krisio la flor delikada de nuestra liberasion
I sovre los guesos keridos i los montes de siniza
A presio de nueva sangre, rebivio nuestra nasion.

Repozad almas keridas de vuestro ultimo suenio.
Vos kayitech. Kon vuestra muerte parissio venser el mal,
Ma kon vuestro ultimo riflo, soplo de nuevo nuestro genio,
I nuestros lavios murmurean: Yitkadach Veyitgadal.

And men, women, and children continue to walk
toward their sad destiny, toward the gas chambers.
They sense in advance the horrible tortures
that await them, and their breathing goes out of perception.

In but a few moments . . . and from the ovens rises a heavy cloud,
gray, in flame, and spreads a strong odor,
and earth does not tremble, nature is not moved,
and the Heavens do not quiver at a just rage.

Thus vanished six million brethren.
The thousand-armed hydra swallowed them pitilessly:
the assassin did his work and the German people,
as if they were not guilty, today enjoy their freedom.

The whole world participated in the macabre spectacle
without trying to save, to help, to punish,
without being moved by a whole nation dead,
without giving signs of repentance or even denial.

But over the death camps and from that gray cloud
grew the delicate flower of our liberation;
and over the beloved bones and mountains of ash,
at the cost of new blood, our nation was restored.

Rest, beloved souls, from your last sleep.
You have fallen. With your death, evil seemed to have conquered,
but with your last breath, you have given life to our genius
and our lips murmur: "Yitgadal veyitkadash."[22]

Saloniko

No. No es esta la sivdad onde vide el dia
No son estos los hombres ke konosi en mi tchikes.
No es este el sol ke entonses ardia,
Ni es este el sielo ke me intchia de boratches.

I yo kreo bivir en una otra planeta
Onde en kada paso me parese a mi ver
Solombras ke defilan—en un numero sin kuenta
I sus vista me aze profondamente ezmover.

Entre eyas yo kreo ver las konosidas figuras
De mis viejos, mis ermanos, de amigos sin kontar
Entre eyas miles son las inosentes kriaturas,
—luzes puras ke las bestias no hezitaron a amatar.

. . . Eyos me siguen en el dia, me presigen en la notche
Onde ke vaya, yo los veo sin ke otros los puedan ver
A mis orejas parviene sus djimido atrotche,
El mizmo ke antes anios no pudo ninguno ezmover.

"Hombre! Onde estavas?" demandan eyos, "dimos kuando
Fuemos todos arastados en este mizmo lugar,
Kuando fuemos deportados, kuando los zonder-komando
Viejos i tchikos en los gazes nos izieron aogar?

"Dimos, onde estavas kuando, flakos i atemados,
Unflados por la ambre, asekados por la sed,
Fuemos rojados en los ornos i eramos ansi kemados
I los djilates degoyaron sin ninguna mersed?

"Onde estava el mundo ke se dize sivilizado?
Onde estavan los puevlos ke gereavan por libertad?
Alora ke los miliones en sus suplisio embrazado
Desparesian en el umo—viktimas de ferosidad.

"Onde esta el pintor ke pintara la tragedia?
Onde esta el poeta ke endetchara por nos?"
Nase el dia, viene la notche i espunta un nuevo dia
I el mundo espera siempre ke se levante akeya boz,

Salonika

No. This is not the city where I first saw light;
These are not the men I knew in my infancy.
This is not the sun that shone then,
Nor this the sky that intoxicated me.

And I think that I live on another planet,
Where at every step I seem to see
Shadows parade in endless numbers,
And their sight moves me profoundly.

Among them I seem to recognize the well-known faces
Of my countless elders, brethren, and friends;
Among them are those of thousands of innocent children,
Bright stars that the beasts did not hesitate to kill.

. . . They follow me by day, they haunt me by night;
Wherever I go I see them when no one else can.
Their excruciating laments reach my ears;
Years ago they could not touch anyone's.

"Man! Where were you?" they ask. "Tell us:
When we were all arrested in this same city,
When we were deported, when the Sonderkommandos
Suffocated our old and young in the gas?

"Tell us: where were you when, feeble and exhausted,
Swollen by hunger, dried with thirst,
We were hurled into the ovens and thus burned,
And the executioners slaughtered with no mercy?

"Where was the world that is considered to be civilized?
Where were the nations that were fighting for freedom?
When millions in their blazing torture
Vanished in smoke, victims of ferocity.

"Where is the artist who will paint the tragedy?
Where is the poet who will mourn us?"
The day begins, night falls, and a new day dawns,
And the world still waits for that voice,

Akeya boz ke djimira por nuestra suerte i vengansa
Demandara por el krimen ke no ay paga para el,
Akeya boz ke en sus notas puedra meter toda la ansia
I la angustia ke fue akeya del puevlo martiryo de Israel.

Ansi pasan las solombras en una fila longa i siento
Sus pasos sovre el asfalto i sus lavios palpitar
I sus kecha estremisiente se konfonde kon el viento
Sin ke pueda el entanto sus djimido arestar.

I yo ando mi kamino sin topar una repuesta
A las kruela demandas i a la djusta folor
En mi alma se desperta una violente tempesta
I yo siento ke mi kuerpo teterea de yelor.

Sovre las sinizas santas del malditcho Birknau
Sovre las muntanias de guesos de los kampos de eksterminasion
Vente anios despues, grande es la luz del rayo
Ke espunto por afirmar la eternidad de la nasion.

Hay vekayam es Israel, bive i firme i nos konsola
de la horrivle perioda la sigureza de saver
Ke mas ninguna fuersa, ke mas ninguna ola
No puedra aravdonarmos, no mos ara despareser.

Salonico, Agosto 1966

The voice that will bemoan our fate and will demand
Vengeance for the crime that has no expiation;
That voice that, in its accounts, would include all the anxiety
And affliction that befell the martyred people of Israel.

So the shadows pass in a long file and I hear
The steps on the asphalt and their lips palpitate,
And their terrifying laments mix with the wind,
The wind that is powerless to drown out the groans.

And I walk along without finding any answer
To the cruel questions and to the just rage.
In my soul a violent tempest awakes
And I feel my body shiver with cold.

On the blessed ashes of cursed Birkenau,
On the mountains of bones of the extermination camps,
Twenty years later, great is the light of the sunbeam
That dawned to affirm the eternity of the nation.

Hay vekayam[23] is Israel; it lives, it is unshaken, and it consoles us
For the time of terror. Secure, we know
That no other force, that no other wave,
Will be able to destroy us and make us vanish.

Salonika, August 1966

ENRIQUE SAPORTA Y BEJA

A native of Salonika, Enrique Saporta y Beja moved to Paris as a youth and continued to study the literature of his people, the Sephardim, and to do research, especially on proverbs. Before his death in 1984 he was preparing for publication the third edition of *Refranero Sefardí* (Sephardic proverbs). He also wrote on the Jews of Salonika in *Selanik i sus Djidyos* (Salonika and her Jews). Several of his unpublished manuscripts deal with the names given to Sephardic children and with the traditions of the Jews in his native city. The poem on the Holocaust included here questions what became of his people.

Que sont-ils devenus?
Question avec reponses

—Que sont devenus nos parents?
  Ils ont été déportés en rangs!

—Que sont devenus nos pères?
  De la chair que l'on opère!

—Que sont devenues nos mères?
  Elles ont mangé des herbes amères!

—Qu'a-t-on fait de nos frères?
  Torturés par le feu et le fer!

—Qu'est-il arrivé à nos soeurs?
  Violées par les ravisseurs!

—Que sont devenus nos garçons?
  On les a changés en savons!

—Que sont devenues nos filles?
  Renversées comme un jeu de quilles!

—Que sont devenus nos bébés?
  La vermine les a absorbés!

—Que sont devenus nos amis?
  Massacrés par nos ennemis!

—Dieu du ciel, Dieu de bonté,
  Comment as-tu permis ces cruautés?
  Comment n'as tu pas empêché
  La solution définitive,
  Et avoir laissé faucher
  Tant de Juifs et tant de Juives?

—Mais quoique blessés en plusieurs endroits,
  nous n'avons pas perdu la foi en TOI.

What Has Become of Them?
Questions with Replies

(Translated by Rosemary Lévy Zumwalt)

—What has become of our parents?
  They were deported in ranks!

—What has become of our fathers?
  Flesh that is operated on!

—What has become of our mothers?
  They have eaten bitter herbs!

—What have they done with our brothers?
  Tortured by fire and steel!

—What has happened to our sisters?
  Violated by ravishers!

—What has become of our sons?
  They have been made into soap!

—What has become of our daughters?
  Knocked down like a set of ninepins!

—What has become of our babies?
  Vermin have eaten them!

—What has become of our friends?
  Massacred by our enemies!

—God in Heaven, God of goodness,
  How have You allowed these cruelties?
  How have You not prevented
  The Final Solution
  And have allowed the mowing down
  Of so many Jewish men and women?

—But even though wounded in many places,
  We have not lost faith in You.

JACQUES TARABOULOS

Presently retired in Jerusalem, Jacques Taraboulos was born in Cairo, Egypt, and is a graduate of the Collegio Rabbinico of Rhodes. He continued his religious studies at the École Rabbinique de Paris and spent many years in Elizabethville, Belgian Congo (now Zaire), where he collaborated with Robert Joseph Cohen on the publication of the series *Etudes Juives*. He has published several articles on the Jews in the Middle Ages and modern times. His intellectual pursuits include research on the Second Temple and the religions of the Middle East. The poems "L'holocauste" and "La Neila" were published in a booklet entitled *Poèmes tristes* (Melancholic poems), pp. 3–11 (there is no indication of the place or date of publication).

La Neila

La fin du jour approche.
Le Livre de Vie et de Mort
est sur le point de se fermer,
et la main de l'Eternel va inscrire
le destin des hommes.

Elle hésite, tremble, s'arrête.
Une voix douce et frêle
un murmure imperceptible,
monte vers les firmaments.
C'est un petit Juif qui prie.
Son âme projetée vers le ciel,
est parvenue jusqu'au Saint des Saints.

Le Hekhal est grand ouvert,
et la Tora est là.
La Science et la Sagesse.
Et un murmure doux,
comme le chant de l'espace,
sort du Hekhal.
L'âme de l'enfant se confond à la Tora
et la Tora prie avec lui.

Pour les morts, les brûlés;
les cadavres qui n'ont pas eu de sépulture;
les ossements qui ont blanchi au soleil.
Pour la misère passée, à venir,
des temps qui furent, et qui seront.
Pour les sanglots du nouveau-né
qui pleure en voyant la lumière;
Pour la douleur des hommes,
des êtres, des fleurs;
de l'herbe frêle piétinée par le passant,
de la rose épanouie que dévore une abeille,
Pour tout ce qui souffre et pleure,
et dont la voix n'atteint pas
l'âme de l'homme.

The Neila[24]

The end of the day approaches.
The Book of Life and Death
is about to be closed,
and the hand of God will inscribe
the destiny of man.

It hesitates, trembles, stops.
A voice, sweet and frail,
an imperceptible murmur,
rises toward the firmament;
it is a young Jew who prays.
His soul, hurled toward Heaven,
reaches the Holy of Holies.

The Ark is opened wide,
and the Torah is there.
Science and Wisdom.
And a sweet murmur,
like a song in space,
emerges from the Ark.
The soul of the child blends with the Torah
and the Torah prays with him.

For the dead, the burned,
the cadavers that had no grave,
the bones that were bleached in the sun;
for the past misery, and that to come,
the time that was, and that will be;
for the sobs of the newborn
who cries on seeing the light;
for the suffering of men,
of creatures, of flowers,
of delicate grass crushed by the passerby,
of the rose in bloom that a bee consumes;
for all that suffers and cries,
and whose voice does not reach
the soul of man.

Et l'Eternel s'attrista de la tristesse
de l'âme,
et la voix de la Tora monta jusqu'à Lui.
Le péché est dans l'homme, O, Père
et le pardon est à Toi,
et l'amour est à Toi,
O grand Dieu d'amour.

Et le Livre de Vie et de Mort,
ne se ferma point à la prière de la Neila.
Car la voix de l'enfant
avait jailli de son coeur;
et comme l'eau d'un ruisseau
va rejoindre la rivière,
son âme avait rejoint la Tora.
Et la Tora est dans Dieu,
et la Tora est Dieu.

1945

And the Eternal grew sad from the sadness
of the soul,
and the voice of the Torah rose up to Him.
The sin is in man, O Father,
and forgiveness is Yours,
and love is Yours,
O Great God of Love.

And the Book of Life and Death
did not close at all with the prayer of the Neila,
because the voice of the child
burst from his heart
and, as the water of a stream
goes to join the river,
his soul had rejoined with the Torah,
and the Torah is in God,
and the Torah is God.

1945

L'holocauste

Ils viennent par vague, les enfants,
vêtus de bleu, de blanc.
Ils sont bruns, blonds,
cuits déjà au soleil de la terre.
Ils viennent se retrouver,
dans les petites âmes de ceux de leur âge,
arrachées à la vie,
par des mains impures et maudites.
Douces victimes de la révolte des Teutons
contre la colonisation millénaire de Rome.

Ils viennent, pleins de vie,
une fleur machonnée au coin de la bouche,
quelques uns débraillés,
tous plein d'entrain,
se retrouver face à l'Histoire, avec leurs disparus.
Ceux qui n'ont jamais cessé de vivre, de vibrer.
Qui vivent et qui vibrent,
sous ces grandes dalles noires,
dans ces tombeaux sans fin,
dont les racines arrivent aux entrailles de la terre.

Une dalle pour Aushwitz.
Une dalle pour Tréblinka.

Et encore une dalle, et une autre encore.
Des milliers de dalles fondues en une seule,
des millions d'âmes fondues dans la lumière
tremblante qui se dégage de ces dalles;
tel de feux follets géants,
dansant devant l'étérnité.

The Holocaust

They come by waves, the children,
dressed in blue, in white.
They are dark, blond,
already burnt by Earth's sun.
They come to meet again,
in the tiny souls of those of their age,
torn away from life
by impure and accursed hands,
sweet victims of the Teutonic revolt
against the thousand-year-old colonization of Rome.

They come, full of life,
a flower clamped in the corner of the mouth,
some untidy,
all full of spirit,
to meet again face to face with History, with their vanished.
Those who have never ceased to live, to pulsate,
who live and who pulsate
under these big black slabs,
in these endless graves,
whose roots reach the bowels of the earth.

A slab for Auschwitz.
A slab for Treblinka.

And another slab, and still another one.
Thousands of slabs reduced to a single one,
millions of souls reduced in the trembling
light that frees itself from these slabs;
like giant will-o'-the-wisps
dancing before Eternity.

Soyez bénis, âmes chères et précieuses,
corps calcinés, fine poudre noire,
que les vents emportent dans leurs tourbillons,
lançant tantôt leurs pleurs
déchirants et lugubres,
tantôt récitant leurs prières
en un murmure doux et triste,
tel le chant de tes forêts, O Jérusalem.
Soyez bénis, à tout jamais, à tout jamais.
Et quand le monde sera perdu dans le néant,
et que la vie se désagrégera dans l'abîme,
vous continuerez à briller,
tel les feux éclatants du soleil de midi.

Et vous, les Justes parmi les Nations,
qui au péril de votre vie,
oubliant la haine que vous inculqua votre foi
et que l'on vous insuffla depuis le berceau,
avez arraché mes frères à la furie des Barbares.
Soyez bénis, soyez bénis.
Vous étiez quelques-uns, une poignée de braves,
des graines robustes et saines,
épanouies au sol de l'amour.

Où étaient les autres?
Les millions d'autres?
Les centaines de millions d'autres?
Leurs voix s'étaient éteintes dans un grand silence,
le grand silence de la haine.
Descendue dans l'arène, Rome voyait avec joie
périr le gladiateur dévoré par le fauve.

Ah! Ils s'étaient fait la main
tout au long des millénaires.
Leurs Sages, complexés de païen,
leur avaient insufflé l'haleine mauvaise
de la fausse conscience,
déclarant tabou, l'amour de l'Homme pour le Juif.

Be blessed, dear and precious souls,
calcinated bodies, fine black dust,
that the winds carry in their dust devils,
sometimes hurling their laments,
heartrending and mournful,
sometimes reciting their prayers
in a gentle and sorrowful murmur,
like the song of your forests, O Jerusalem.
Be blessed, forever and ever, forever and ever.
And when the world is lost in nothingness,
and life breaks up into the abyss,
you will continue to shine
like the bright fires of the noonday sun.

And you, the just among nations,
who at the risk of your life,
forgetting the hatred that your faith had taught you
and that was breathed into you ever since the cradle,
have torn my brothers away from the fury of the barbarians.
Be blessed, be blessed.
You were a few, a handful of brave men,
robust and sound seeds,
full-blown in the soil of love.

Where were the others?
The millions of others?
The hundreds of millions of others?
Their voices died into a great silence,
the great silence of hatred.
Gone down into the arena, Rome saw with joy
the gladiator perish, devoured by the wild beast.

Ah! They have played their hand
all through the millennia.
Their sages, muddled by pagan inheritance,
breathed into them the foul breath
of a warped conscience,
declaring human love for the Jew taboo.

Ils s'étaient fait la main tout au long de l'Histoire,
et ils ont continué.
Puissants, dominant le monde,
par le mépris et la calomnie
ils s'étaient fait la main.

Par le vol d'enfants, et le vol des âmes;
par les chairs brûlées de Juifs et de Juives
liés sur des Croix de la Honte,
ils s'étaient fait la main.

L'odeur des chairs brûlées,
était agréable à leurs dieux.
Elle se répandait dans leurs narines
de pierre et de bois,
en un délicieux parfum de témoignage et d'offrande.
Les cris des brûlants vifs,
quelle belle musique aux oreilles de leurs Sages,
quel bel encouragement pour leurs ouailles.

Oeuvre admirable de la . . . "Très Sainte Inquisition."
Opprobe et damnation.
Des Croisés massacrant tous les Juifs sur leur chemin
guidés par le verbe de feu de leurs moines.
Conquérant Jérusalem,
les Croisés y enfermèrent tous les Juifs
dans leurs Synagogues.
Tous.
Sages et ignares, hommes femmes et enfants,
et y mirent le feu.
Tout y passa.
Tout.
Pour la plus grande gloire de leurs dieux.

They have played their hand all along history,
and they have continued.
Powerful, dominating the world,
through contempt and calumny,
they have played their hand.

Through the theft of children and the theft of souls,
through the burned bodies of Jewish men and women,
bound on the Cross of Shame,
they have played their hand.

The smell of the burned bodies
was pleasing to their gods.
It diffused itself in their nostrils
of stone and wood,
in delightful perfume of testimony and offering.
The screams of the alive burning,
what sweet music to the ears of their sages,
what beautiful encouragement for their flock.

Admirable deed that of the . . . "Right Holy Inquisition."
Disgrace and damnation.
Crusaders massacring all the Jews in their path,
guided by the fiery word of their monks.
Conquering Jerusalem,
the Crusaders shut all the Jews
up in their synagogues.
All of them.
Sages and illiterates, men, women, and children,
and they set them on fire.
Everything took place there,
Everything,
For the greater glory of their gods.

Worms. Spiers. Mayence.
Et tant d'autres et tant d'autres,
étoiles de malheur, brillant d'un feu de sang,
n'avez vous point guidé les pas du Grand Maudit?
O Croix de la Honte, couverte de chairs brulées,
n'avez vous point porté en votre sein
la Croix Gammée de la Brute?
O Torquemada, de maudite mémoire,
O Isabelle, chienne de malheur,
O Grand Maudit, Nazis misérables et vils,
puissent vos os se consumer
dans le feu et la honte.

Vos sages et vos chefs;
ceux qui pouvaient arrêter la mort;
et se cachèrent dans le silence assassin.

Ceux qui ordonnèrent et ceux qui exécutèrent;
ceux qui guidèrent et ceux qui obéirent.
Ceux qui enfouirent leur conscience,
sous la fausse conscience de leur confesseur.
Les maîtres et les disciples,
les connus et les inconnus,
leurs nobles et leur racaille;
soyez maudits à tout jamais, à tout jamais.

Pour avoir, tout au long des âges,
déraciné mes âmes douces et frêles,
mes tendres fleurs qui n'ont pas pu s'épanouir,
balbutier, gazouiller, chanter, crier,
remplir le monde de leur chant à la vie,
à l'espoir, à l'amour de l'Eternel.
Puissiez vous disparaître dans l'enfer
de l'oubli et de la honte,
des choses misérables et viles.

Worms, Speyer, Mainz,
and so many other places.
Stars of ill omen, shining with a bloody fire,
have you not guided the steps of the Great Devil?
O Cross of Shame, covered with burned flesh,
have you not borne on your bosom
the Swastika of the Brute?
O Torquemada, of cursed memory,
O Isabella, bitch of misfortune,
O Great Cursed, miserable and worthless Nazis,
may your bones be consumed
in fire and shame.

Your sages and your leaders,
those who could have put an end to death,
they hid themselves in the murderous silence.

Those who gave the orders and those who carried them out,
those who guided and those who obeyed,
those who buried their consciences
under the false conscience of their confessor,
the masters and the disciples,
those known and those unknown,
their noble and their rabble,
be cursed forever and ever, forever and ever.

For having, all through the years,
uprooted my gentle and frail souls,
my tender flowers that have not been able to blossom,
to stammer, to babble, to sing, to cry out,
to fill the world with their songs to life,
to hope, to the love of God.
May you vanish in the hell
of oblivion and disgrace,
of things miserable and vile.

Et toi, O terre de Danemark, qui fus l'exception,
sois à tout jamais bénie au sein de l'Eternel.
Ton Roi, tes filles et tes fils,
tes vivants et tes morts;
et la mer qui lèche tes rivages,
Pour avoir vu tant de bravoure et d'amour.
Puisse la main de l'Eternel être sur toi,
et te garder jusqu'à la fin des temps.

Et nous Juifs qui vivons sur la terre,
faisons en le serment:
Point d'oubli pour les lâches puissants,
qui vous massacrèrent par le feu et le gaz.
Point d'oubli pour les faux sages,
qui lâchement se cachèrent dans le Grand Silence.
Et pour vous, Juifs de par le monde,
pour vous, Justes parmi les Nations,
notre amour et l'offrande de notre vie.

Et pour toi, O Jérusalem la belle,
pour ta couronne de pins et d'oliviers,
pour tes monts, tes vallées
et l'ombre de tes bois,

Pour toi, O Israël,
pour la vie qui renaît en ton sein
jaillissant des pleurs et du déséspoir;
pour le sourire de tes enfants,
l'arrogance de tes jeunes,
le visage épanoui de tes filles saines et belles;
pour le bonnet aguichant
posé sur la tête de tes soldates;
pour le regard timide et brave de tes soldats;
pour les papillotes de tes pieux
se balançant au vent;

And you, O land of Denmark, that was the exception,
be forever and ever blessed in the bosom of the Eternal.
Your king, your daughters and your sons,
your living and your dead,
and the sea that touches your shores,
for having seen so much bravery and love,
may the hand of God be upon you,
and keep you until the end of time.

And we Jews who live on earth,
let us take an oath:
Never to forget the powerful cowards
who massacred by fire and gas.
Never to forget the false sages
who like cowards hid themselves in the Great Silence.
And for you, Jews the world over,
for you, Just among nations,
our love and the offering of our life.

And for you, O Jerusalem the beautiful,
for your crown of pine trees and olive trees,
for your mountains and your valleys,
and the shade of your forests,

For you, O Israel,
for the life that is born again in your bosom
gushing from tears and despair;
for the smile of your children,
the pride of your youth,
the faces in full bloom of your healthy and beautiful daughters;
for the jaunty caps
resting on the heads of your female soldiers;
for the timid and brave look of your soldiers;
for the earlocks of your pious,
blowing in the air;

pour les caftans fatigués de tes "Cent Portes";
pour les pantalons aux broderies fanées
de tes Yéménites;
pour ton Jourdain rapide et nerveux;
pour tes orangeraies innondant tout
de leur parfum moelleux et chaud;
pour tes usines, tes prés,
tes champs, tes semailles;
pour tes citées fières qui naissent dans les sables,
poèmes de ciment et de fer tordu
se lançant vers le ciel;
pour ton soleil et ta lumière,
O pays bien-aimé,
pour ton Mur vénérable, vieilli par le temps,
gardien nostalgique des Lieux du Temple;
pour tout cela,
et pour tout ce que je ne parviens pas à dire,
nous t'aimerons à jamais, O Israël . . .

1973

for the caftans wearied of your "Hundred Gates";[25]
for the bloused embroidered trousers
of your Yemenites;
for your Jordan, swift and strong;
for your orange groves, overwhelming everything
with their perfume, intoxicating and warm;
for your factories, your meadows,
your fields, your sowings and harvests;
for your proud cities that spring up in the sands,
poems of cement and twisted iron
thrusting toward Heaven;
for your sun and your light,
O beloved country,
for your venerated Wall, aged by time,
nostalgic guardian of the Place of the Temple;
for all of that,
and for all that I am not able to say,
we will love you forever and ever, O Israel . . .

1973

JENNIE ADATTO TARABULUS

In 1954 Jennie Adatto moved to Israel from Seattle, Washington, her birthplace, to marry David Tarabulus, a native of Turkey who, as a young man, had moved with his family to Xanthi, northern Thrace, in Greece. She informed me that before the war her husband had "fatefully left for Baghdad to work temporarily. His mother, father, two brothers, sister-in-law, and an infant niece perished in the camps, and the letters sent to Greece by David Tarabulus were returned stamped 'Moved to Cracow, address unknown'." After his death, Jennie Tarabulus felt compelled to visit his city, now depleted of Jews. She was saddened by the thought that, like all the Greek Jews, his family was also forgotten in the Holocaust, which, in her words, "somehow is always associated only with the Jews of Eastern Europe. I wanted to memorialize their existence." Upon her return to Israel she wrote the poem reproduced here as part of a documentary program aired by Kol Israel Radio on "The Greek Jews in the Holocaust."

Oh mes hermanos

Como se fueron
como se fueron
Oh mis hermanos
Hermanos en Grecia

De Salonika y de Laressa y de Cavallo
de Xanthe y Rhodos y de la Drama
y de Atena y Comotino
y de las islas
Las islas de Grecia

Si ya sabemos como guerraron
como partisanes en Macedonia
y ya hoimos del unico que quedo bivo,
al coraje revolto de Auswitz '44.

Oh mes hermanos
Solos muriendo
En tierra estrange un muerte cruelo
no vos olvido
no vos olvido
Tus corasones son con nosotros
siempre por siempre en tierra Sancta
La tierra sancta—Jerusalem.

O My Brethren!

How they perished!
How they perished!
O my brethren,
Brethren from Greece!

From Salonika and from Larisa and from Kavalla,
from Xanthi and Rhodes and from Drama
and from Athens and Komotino
and from the islands,
the islands of Greece.

Yes, we already know how they fought
as partisans in Macedonia,
and we have heard of the only one to remain alive[26]
from the brave revolt of Auschwitz '44.

O my brethren!
Dying alone,
a cruel death in a foreign land.
I do not forget you;
I do not forget you.
Your hearts are with us all,
forever and ever in a holy land,
the Holy Land—Jerusalem.

GROUP COMPOSITIONS

These song-poems were composed by groups of survivors:

"Here in This Land" was the work of a group of young women from Rhodes while in the concentration camps, 1944–45. I received two versions from Mrs. Violette Fintz. The first stanza of the second version (not used here) contains five lines, the fourth of which was crossed out. It reads: "Visi impalliditi, tristi ed avvility" (I lived pale, sad, and discouraged).

"In Polish Lands" was written by the Grupo de los Reskatados de los Kampos de Alemania (Group of Liberated Inmates from the German Camps), also known as Koro Saloniko, during internment in Auschwitz. The original song and melody were taken from a popular Judeo-Spanish song, "Arvoles yoran por luvia" (Trees cry for rain). The members, Salomon and Renée Bivas and Haim and Esther Rafael, now live in Israel. They contribute their services to organizations memorializing the tragedy.

"A Little Jewess I Was" and "Pitch Dark Is Our Life" were written by survivors from Salonika and were made available to me by Dimitri N. Molfetas, former president of the American Friends of the Jewish Museum of Greece.

Qui in questa terra

Qui in questa terra
Triste e maledetta
Vivono tanti figli d'Israel
Pensano ai cari che 'stan tanto lontan

O Gran Dio vogliam la libertà
Dai nostri vogliamo ritornar
Stanchi e sfiniti noi
Attendiamo la liberazion

O Gran Dio rispondi anche Tu
Non vogliamo più restare quaggiù
Noi promettiamo con sicura fede
I nostri cari un giorno vendicar

Here in This Land

Here in this land,
Sad and accursed,
Live so many children of Israel,
Thinking of their dear ones who are so far away.

O Great God! We want freedom;
We want to return to our people.
Tired and worn out,
We await liberation.

O Great God! Answer, even You.
We do not want to remain here any longer.
We promise with sure and certain faith
One day to avenge our dear ones.

En tierras de Polonia

Arvoles yoran por luvias
I muntanias por ayre
Ansi yoran los mis ojos
Por ti kerida madre
Ansi yoran los mis ojos
Por ti kerida madre

Torno i digo ke va ser de mi
En tierras de Polonia
Me tengo ke murir

Blanka sos blanka vistes
Blanka es la tu figura
Blankas flores kayen de ti
De la tu ermozura
Blankas flores kayen de ti
De la tu ermozura

Torno i digo ke va ser de mi
En tierras de Polonia
Me tengo ke murir

In Polish Lands

Trees cry for rain
And mountains for air.
So cry my eyes
For you, dear Mother;
So cry my eyes
For you, dear Mother.

I turn and I ask what will become of me.
In Polish lands
I am destined to die.

White you are and white you wear;
White is your face.
White flowers fall from you,
From your beauty;
White flowers fall from you,
From your beauty.

I turn and I ask what will become of me.
In Polish lands
I am destined to die.

Ἑβραιοπούλα ἤμουνα

Ἑβραιοπούλα ἤμουνα
Τ' ἀστεράκι φόρεσα
Μᾶς πλακῶσαν τὰ κοθώνια
Καὶ μὰς πῆγαν στὴν Πολώνια

Στὴν Πολώνια πήγαμε
Πώ, Πώ, Πώ, τί πάθαμε,
Μᾶς κουρέψαν τά μαλλιά
Καὶ μὰς ντύσαν ἀνδρικά

Τὸ πρωὶ στὸ Ἀουφστέεν
Βγαίναμε στὸ Τσέλ-Ἀπέλ
Πάντα πέντε στὴ σειρὰ
(Ἄχ! μανούλα μου γλυκειά)
Πάντα πέντε στὴ γραμμή
(Ἄχ! μανούλα μου χρυσή)

Στὸ λουτρὸ μᾶς πηγαίνανε
Γιὰ ψῶρα μᾶς κυττάζανε
Κι' ἡ καρδιὰ μᾶς τίκ τίκ τάκ
Μὴν τυχὸν στὸ γκάζ μᾶς πᾶν

Στὴ δουλεία πηγαίνουμε
Μὲ ἀνέμους καὶ βροχές
κι' ἄν σιγὰ δουλεύουμε
τὸ μπαστούνι βλέπουμε

A Little Jewess I Was

(Translated by Olga Augustinos)

A little Jewess I was
I put on my little star
The wretches fell on us
And took us to Poland

To Poland we went
Oh! what we had to suffer
They shaved off our hair
And dressed us in men's clothes

In the morning upon awakening
We came out for roll call
Always five in a row
(Oh! my sweet mother)
Always five in a row
(Oh! my precious mother)

They took us to the showers
they searched for lice
Thump, thump, our hearts went
Will they take us to the gas?

Off to work we go
Come wind or come rain
And if our work is slow
We feel the cane's blow

Μαύρη μωρὲ μαύρ᾽ εἶν᾽ ἡ ζωὴ ποὺ κάνομε

Μαύρη μωρὲ μαύρ᾽ εἶν᾽ ἡ ζωὴ ποὺ κάνομε
Μὲ φόβο τρῶμε τὸ ψωμί, μὲ φόβο περπατᾶμε

Στὴ βρύση μωρέ, στὴ βρύση νὰ πάω δὲν μπορῶ,
Παντοῦ μοῦ λέει ὁ σκοπὸς "εἶσαι φυλακισμένη,
      γερμανοκρατουμένη"

Δὲν ἔκλεψα μωρέ, δὲν ἔκλεψα οὔτε σκότωσα
Ἑβραιοπούλα ἤμουνα, γιαυτὸ μὲ φυλακίσαν, στὸ Ἀουσβίτς μὲ
      κλείσαν

Χαλάλι μωρέ, χαλάλι στὰ Ἐγγλεζάκια μας
Αὐτὰ θὰ μᾶς γλυτώσουν καὶ θὰ μᾶς λευτερώσουν πιό μέσα θὰ μᾶς
      χώσουν.

Pitch Dark Is Our Life

(Translated by Olga Augustinos)

Pitch dark is our life.
In fear we eat our bread; in fear we walk.

To the fountain, the fountain I cannot go.
The guard always warns me: "A prisoner you are held by the
    Germans."

I didn't steal, didn't steal or kill.
A little Jewess I was; for this they jailed me and locked me up in
    Auschwitz.

Bless, bless the English lads.
They will save us, they will liberate us, and deeper in they will
    push us.

NOTES

1. This version of the poem was given to me by Mrs. Stella Hasson, a survivor of Auschwitz who was born on Rhodes, as were Mrs. Violette Fintz (now of Cape Town, South Africa) and her sister, Mrs. Sara Menasche (Brussels, Belgium). At the time, Mrs. Hasson was not aware who the authors were, claiming that the poem was written by deportees from Rhodes while they were being transported to different camps in Poland and Germany. A slightly different version was published by Adolfo Arditti in *Aki Yerushalayim* (p. 26), along with four other poems on the Holocaust, also written by Sephardim. Three of them—"Echados adientro del fuego" and "Siniza i fumo," by Avner Perets, and "Siete dias enserados," by Haim David—appear in this book by permission of the authors and Moshe Shaul, the editor of *Aki Yerushalayim*; the fourth poem, "El gayiko de Birkenau" by Joy Anderson, is not included here. The English version of the poem contributed by Mrs. Hasson is a literal translation: there was no attempt to render the monotonous rhythm of the original more lyrical, for the repetitive martial beat created in the original poem requires an imitation of the deathlike rhythm. The syntactical schemes found in the two parts of this rhythm, as reflected in the accompanying musical arrangement, were transcribed from the vocal rendition obtained in 1958.

2. This refers to the air force headquarters in downtown Rhodes, not to the airport.

3. The instructions of Evelyne Kadouche were that no changes be made in the format of the poem nor in the approved English translation. However, I would like to propose the following changes in the English translation:
line 9, for "fleeing down," read "hurled down";
line 25, for "cherguy," read "a desert wind";
line 30, for "analphabet assassination," read "assassinated illiterate."

4. I believe that the author must be referring to Ponary, a village ten kilometers from Vilna, where thousands of Jews were killed in death pits.

5. "Yitgadal veyitkadash shemei raba" means "Exalted and hallowed be the name of God."

6. "Barouh Dayan Aémeth" can also be translated as "Blessed is the Judge of Truth."

7. Bet Amigdash is the Holy Temple in Jerusalem.

8. "Bet Hahaya" means "house of the living." It is customary to call the cemetery the house of the living rather than the house of the dead.

9. This commentary does not appear in the manuscript given to me in Kavalla by Moise Pessah, the poet's nephew. The poem is dedicated to "the Jews of Salonica."

10. "Yir vaem belsrael" means "City and Mother of Israel."

11. See note 7.

12. My sources inform me that "Hasmonay" must refer to Mattathias the Hasmonean, also known as Mattathia, the son of Johanan the High Priest.

13. "Mamhelet coanim ve goy kadoch" means "A kingdom of priests and holy nation."

14. "Eretz Israel" means "Land of Israel."

15. Tisha Beav is the day set aside to commemorate the destruction of the Temple in Jerusalem.

16. The imbat is a cooling Etesian wind in the Levant, blowing northerly during the summer over the eastern Mediterranean.

17. The zephyr is a soft, warm breeze from the west.

18. "Zéhout Avoth" means "merit of the Fathers."

19. "Ancient of Days" refers to God, to the deity, and it is found in several works, among them Daniel 7:9, 13, 22.

20. "Malahe a-sharet" means "Angels who serve God."

21. Yom Hachoa, the Day of Remembrance, commemorates the tragedy of the Holocaust. This poem was first read in Judeo-Spanish on Kol Israel Radio, "Special Emission," on April 28, 1952, and was published on April 24, 1966, in *La Verdad* of Tel Aviv.

22. See note 5.

23. "Hay vekayam" means "living and enduring."

24. The Neila is the closing prayer of Yom Kippur, the Day of Atonement. It is read at the hour when the Book of Life and Death is to be closed by the Almighty. This poem was published under the title "La Neila, quatrième et dernière prière du jour de Kippur" in *Etudes Juives* (April 1949).

25. "Hundreds of Gates" refers to the Meah Shearim in Jerusalem where the Hasidic Jews live.

26. In a letter dated December 9, 1944, Mrs. Jennie Tarabulus informed me:

> The "unico" [the only one] refers to the one survivor of the revolters caught in the crematorium 3 as the Nazis bombed and burned them out in battle that lasted a few hours. His name was Itzhah Venezia, from Salonica (who held Italian citizenship). As the crematorium walls crashed he managed to crawl to an iron barbed wire fence enclosing the area, found an opening, crawled through that and into the crematorium 3 area where the survivors were being shot. However, a kapo from the neighboring crematorium 4, who knew him, asked the SS guard to release him as he needed extra helpers. So Venezia survived. However, he died of exhaustion later on in Ebenze camp where the Germans, retreating, marched their prisoners as they fled from the Russians. There were eyewitnesses among the survivors. I got this information from a book published here in Israel "Salonika."

Bibliography

Ainsztein, Reuben. *Jewish Resistance in Nazi-Occupied Eastern Europe.* New York: Barnes & Nobles, 1974.

Alexander, Edward. *Resonance of Dust: Essays on Holocaust Literature and Jewish Fate.* Columbus: Ohio State University Press, 1979.

Altabe, David F. "Four Poems on the Holocaust." *The Sephardic Brother,* no. 1, 19 (Spring 1978), 3–4.

Alteras, Isaac. "Holocaust in the Middle East: Iraq and the Mufti of Jerusalem." In *Sephardim and the Holocaust,* ed. Solomon Gaon and M. Mitchell Serels. New York: Yeshiva Univesity, 1987, pp. 101–9.

Arditi, Adolfo. "Sinko poemas sovrel Olokosto." *Aki Yerushalayim,* no. 21 6 (April 1984), 23–28.

Asseo, Henriette. "Du miel aux cendres." *Les Temps Modernes,* October-November 1979, pp. 842–45.

Avni, Haim. "Rescue Attempts during the Holocaust." Proceedings of the Second Yad Vashem International Historical Conference, April 1974. Jerusalem: Yad Vashem, 1977, pp. 555–90.

———. *Spain, the Jews and Franco,* trans. Emanuel Shimoni. Philadelphia: The Jewish Publication Society of America, 1982.

———. "Spanish Nationals in Greece and Their Fate during the Holocaust." *Yad Vashem Studies,* 8 (1970), 31–68.

Bauer, Yehuda. *The Holocaust in Historical Perspective.* Seattle: University of Washington Press, 1978.

———. *The Jewish Emergence from Powerlessness.* Toronto: University of Toronto Press, 1979.

———. *They Chose Life: Jewish Resistance in the Holocaust.* New York: American Jewish Committee, 1978.

Beker, Ruth. "Don't Show Me." In *Voices within the Ark,* ed. Howard Schwartz and Anthony Rudolf. New York: Avon Books, 1980, pp. 772–73.

Ben, Joseph. "Jewish Leadership in Greece during the Holocaust." In *Patterns of Jewish Leadership in Nazi Europe, 1933-1945.* Proceedings of the Third Yad Vashem International Historical Conference, April 1977. Jerusalem: Yad Vashem, 1979, pp. 335–52.

Ben Ruby, Itzkah. *El sekreto del mudo,* 2d ed. Tel Aviv: Lidor, 1953.

Benardete, Mair José. *Hispanic Culture and Character of the Sephardic Jews.* New York: Hispanic Institute, 1952.

Berenbaum, Michael. *The Vision of the Void: Theological Reflections on the Works of Elie Wiesel.* Middleton, Conn.: Wesleyan University Press, 1979.

Berkovits, Eliezer. *Faith after the Holocaust.* New York: KATV, 1973.

Besso, Henry V. *Dramatic Literature of the Sephardic Jews of Amsterdam in the XVIIth and XVIIIth Centuries.* New York: Hispanic Institute, 1947.

————. "Recent Theories on the Origins of the Sephardim." In *Sephardim and a History of Or Veshalom,* ed. Sol Beton. Monroe, Ga.: Walton Press, 1981, pp. 13–18.

Beton, Sol, ed. *Sephardim and a History of Or Veshalom.* Monroe, Ga.: Walton Press, 1981.

Bialik, Chaim Nahman. *Selected Poems,* trans. Maurice Samuel. New York: Union of American Hebrew Congregations, 1972.

Borgel, Robert. *Etoile jaune et croix gammée: Récit d'une servitude.* Tunis: Editions Artypo, 1944.

Brenner, Reeve Robert. *Faith and Doubt of the Holocaust Survivors.* New York: Macmillan, 1980.

Brown, Robert McAfee. *Elie Wiesel: Messenger to All Humanity.* Notre Dame, Ind.: University of Notre Dame Press, 1983.

Browne, Luis. *How Odd of God: An Introduction to the Jews.* New York: Macmillan, 1934.

Cargas, Harry James, ed. *Responses to Elie Wiesel.* New York: Persea Books, 1978.

Carpi, Daniel. "Nuovi documenti per la storia dell'Olocausto in Grecia— L'atteggiamento degli italiani (1941-1943)." *Michael,* 8 (1981), 119–200.

Chalom, Marcel. *Poèmes Juifs.* Istanbul: Becid Basimevi, 1949.

Chedal, André. *Le muet d'Auschwitz.* Paris: La Pensée Universelle, 1973.

Cohen, Arthur A. *The Tremendum.* New York: Crossroad, 1981.

Dawidowicz, Lucy S. *The War against the Jews, 1933-1945.* New York: Holt, Rinehart and Winston, 1975.

"Endecha, despues de la catastrofa de Salonica." *Le Judaïsme Sephardi,* April 1959, p. 815.

Ezrahi, Sidran DeKoven. *By Words Alone: The Holocaust in Literature.* Chicago: University of Chicago Press, 1980.

Eyre, Roland. *Roland Eyre on the Long Search.* New York: William Collins, 1979.

Feig, Konnilyn G. *Hitler's Death Camps: The Sanity of Madness.* New York: Holmes & Meier, 1981.

Fine, Ellen S. *Legacy of Night: The Literary Universe of Elie Wiesel.* Albany: State University of New York Press, 1982.

Franco, Hizkia. *Les martyrs Juifs de Rhodes et de Cos.* Elizabethville: n.p., 1952.

Florentin, Rafael Yosef. *Kozas pasadas.* Kavalla: n.p., 1929.

Friedlander, Albert H. *Out of the Whirlwind: A Reader of Holocaust Literature.* New York: Schocken Books, 1968.

Friedman, Saul S. *Amcha: An Oral Testament of the Holocaust.* Washington, D.C.: University Press of America, 1981.

Galanté, Abraham. *Histoire des Juifs de Rhodes, Cos, etc.* Istanbul: Fratelli Haim, 1935.

Gaon, Solomon. "The Role of Spain in Protecting Sephardic Jews in France during the Holocaust." In *Sephardim and the Holocaust,* ed. Solomon Gaon and M. Mitchell Serels. New York: Yeshiva University, 1987, pp. 26–32.

Gaon, Solomon, and M. Mitchell Serels, eds. *Sephardim and the Holocaust.* New York: Yeshiva University, 1987.

Gilbert, Martin. *Atlas of the Holocaust.* New York: Macmillan, 1982.

———. *The Fate of the Jews in Nazi Europe.* New York: Mayflower Books, 1979.

———. *The Holocaust: A History of Jews of Europe during the Second World War.* New York: Holt, Rinehart and Winston, 1945.

Heschel, Abraham Joshua. "The Meaning of This Hour." In *Out of the Whirlwind: A Reader of Holocaust Literature,* Albert H. Friedlander. New York: Schocken Books, 1968, pp. 488–92.

Hilberg, Raul. *The Destruction of the European Jews.* Chicago: Quadrangle Books, 1967.

Jewish Museum of Greece. *The Jews of Greece,* ed. Nikos Stavroulakis. Oak Brook, Ill.: American Friends of the Jewish Museum of Greece, 1984.

Katz, Robert. *Black Sabbath: A Journey through a Crime against Humanity.* Toronto: Macmillan, 1969.

Klarsfeld, Serge. *Additif au mémorial des Juifs de France / Le procès de Cologne.* Paris: Klarsfeld, n.d.

———. *Le mémorial de la déportation des Juifs de France.* Paris: Klarsfeld, n.d.

Konnilyn, G. Feig. *Hitler's Death Camps: The Sanity of Madness.* New York: Holmes & Meier, 1981.

Kren, George M., and Leon Rappoport. *The Holocaust and the Crisis of Human Behavior.* New York: Holmes & Meier, 1980.

Levin, Nora. *The Holocaust: The Destruction of European Jewry, 1933-45.* New York: Thomas Y. Crowell, 1968.

Lévy, Isaac Jack. "Holocaust Poetry: The Forgotten Sephardim," *The Sephardic Scholar,* ser. 4 (1979-82), 111–24. Reprinted with revisions and new poems in *Center for Holocaust Studies,* nos. 2-3, 3 (1987), 12–17.

———. "Sephardic Ballads and Songs in the United States." Master's thesis, University of Iowa, 1959. A limited edition of fifty copies was published under a grant from the American Sephardic Federation.

———. "The Sephardim: End of an Odyssey." In *Sephardim and a History of Or Veshalom,* ed. Sol Beton. Monroe, Ga.: Walton Press, 1981, pp. 1–12.

Meltzer, Milton. *Never to Forget: The Jews of the Holocaust.* New York: Harper and Row, 1976.

Menasche, Albert. *Birkenau: Auschwitz II.* New York: Albert Martin, 1947.

Molho, Michael. *In Memoriam,* 2d ed. Thessalonique: n.p., 1973.

Morguez Algrante, Esther. *9 Eylûl: Poesias.* Istanbul: Baski Baykar, 1975.

Müller, Filip. *Eyewitness Auschwitz: Three Years in the Gas Chambers*. New York: Stein and Day, 1979.

Nes-El, Moshe. "Los Judíos Sefaradíes y el Holocausto." *Sefárdica*, no. 3, 2 (1985); 147–55.

Novitch, Miriam. *Le passage des Barbares*, 2d ed. Lohamei Haghetaot: Ghetto Fighters House, 1982.

Oren, Nissan. "The Bulgarian Exception: a Reassessment of the Salvation of the Jewish Community." *Yad Vashem Studies*, 7 (1968), 83–106.

Papo, José. *En attendant l'aurore: Activité de la communauté Séphardie de Paris pendant l'occupation, 1940-1945*. Paris: n.p., 1945.

Perahia, Yehuda. "Endecha, Despues de la catastrofa de Salonica." *Le Judaïsme Sephardi*, April 1959, p. 815.

Perets, Avner. *Siniza i fumo*. Jerusalem: Edision Bilingue, 1986.

Reuven, Chelomo. "Poema: Saloniko," *El Tiempo*, August 16, 1966.

———. "Yom Hachoa," *La Verdad*, no. 1560 (April 24, 1966).

Rose, Peter I. "Review of *The Abandonment of the Jews: America and the Holocaust* by David S. Wyman." *The Christian Science Monitor*, January 15, 1985, pp. 23–24.

Ross, Robert W. *So It Was True: The American Press and the Nazi Persecution of the Jews*. Minneapolis: University of Minnesota Press, 1980.

Runes, Dagobert D. *Let My People Go*. New York: Philosophical Library, 1974.

Sabile, Jacques. "Les Juifs de Tunisie sous l'occupation, les journées tragiques." *Le Monde Juif*, 14 (December 1948), 13–15.

Schwartz, Howard, and Anthony Rudolph, eds. *Voices within the Ark*. New York: Avon Books, 1980.

Senech, Hanna. "Blessed Is the Match." In *Blessed Is the Match: The Story of Jewish Resistance*, trans. Marie Syrkin. London: Victor Gollancz, 1948.

Sephiha, Haim Vidal. *L'Agonie des Judéo-Espagnols*. Paris: Editions Entente, 1977.

———. "1943–1983: Komo olvidar selanik?," *Vidas Largas*, no. 2 (April 1983), 44–46. The poems in this article were written by Henriette Asseo in French and translated into Judeo-Spanish by the editor.

Serels, M. Mitchell. "The Non-European Holocaust: The Fate of Tunisian Jewry." In *Sephardim and the Holocaust*, ed. Solomon Gaon and M. Mitchell Serels. New York: Yeshiva University, 1987, pp. 110–27.

Sevillas, Errikos. *Athens-Auschwitz*, trans. Nikos Stavroulakis. Athens: Lycabettus Press, 1983.

Shonfeld, Moshe. *The Holocaust Victims Accuse*. Brooklyn: Netureikarta of U.S.A., 1977.

Stavrianos, L. S. "The Jews of Greece." *Journal of Central European Affairs*, no. 3, 8 (October 1948), 256–81.

Syrkin, Marie. *Blessed Is the Match: The Story of Jewish Resistance*. London: Victor Gollancz, 1948.

Tamir, Vicki. "Bulgaria, a Difference." In *Sephardim and the Holocaust,* ed. Solomon Gaon and M. Mitchell Serels. New York: Yeshiva University, 1987, pp. 33–43.

Taraboulos, Jacques. *Poèmes tristes.* Published by the author, n.d.

Wiesel, Elie. *Ani Maamin: A Song Lost and Found Again.* Bilingual ed., trans. Marion Wiesel. New York: Random House, 1973.

———. *A Jew Today.* New York: Random House, 1978.

———. "The Holocaust as Literary Inspiration." In *Dimensions of the Holocaust: Lectures at Northwestern University.* Evanston, Ill.: Northwestern University Press, 1977, pp. 4–19.

———. "Israel: The Chosen People." In *Roland Eyre on the Long Search,* Roland Eyre. New York: William Collins, 1979, pp. 59–81.

———. *Legends of Our Time.* New York: Holt, Rinehart and Winston, 1968.

Zuccotti, Susan. *The Italians and the Holocaust: Persecution, Rescue, and Survival.* New York: Basic Books, 1987.

Zimmels, H. J. *The Echo of the Nazi Holocaust in Rabbinic Literature.* New York: KATV, 1977.

Author-Title Index

A Note on the Author/Translator

Isaac Jack Lévy was born in Rhodes, Italy (now Greece), and spent the war years in Tangier, Morocco. In 1945 he immigrated to the United States and later enlisted in the U.S. army, serving in this country and in Germany. He received a B.A. from Emory University (1957), an M.A. from the University of Iowa (1959), and a Ph.D. from the University of Michigan (1966). Lévy joined the faculty of the University of South Carolina in 1963, where he is now a professor of Spanish language and literature. The founder of several academic organizations, including the American Society of Sephardic Studies, he has been editor of the *Sephardic Scholar* and the *Hispanic Studies Series.* His research interests include Sephardic ballads, songs, proverbs, poetry, folk religion, and also Holocaust studies. Among his publications are *Sephardic Ballads and Songs in the United States* and *Prolegomena to the Study of the "Refranero Sefardí."* He is working on a book about the history and traditions of the Jews of Rhodes.